James A. Banks

AND THE EVOLUTION OF
MULTICULTURAL EDUCATION

---

*Implications for Teacher Educators
and Curriculum Development*

Andrew Jackson, Sr.

James A. Banks and the Evolution of Multicultural Education: Implications for Teacher Educators and Curriculum Development

Published by Wheatmark®
610 East Delano Street, Suite 104
Tucson, Arizona 85705 U.S.A.
www.wheatmark.com

ISBN-13: 978-1-58736-719-9
ISBN-10: 1-58736-719-X
Library of Congress Control Number: 2006935415

This book is dedicated to the memory of my parents, Lucius and Essie Mae Jackson, brothers Thomas Lee Jackson and Lucius Jackson, Jr., and my sister, Rebecca.

This book is also dedicated to the memory of all family, friends, relatives, and colleagues who aspired to a better life thru Service Above Self in pursuit of Education, Manhood, Scholarship, Perseverance, Uplift and Respect to Finer Womanhood!

Table of Contents

Foreword

Christine Sleeter
California State University, Monterey Bay

There is an urgent need to improve teachers' preparation to work successfully with diverse students. We know that teachers generally hold higher academic expectations for White or Asian students than for Black or Latino students. White teachers often have more difficulty forming constructive relationships with students of color, particularly African American students, than with White students. Commonly assuming that parents of color do not value education, White teachers are often reluctant to build relationships with them, or simply do not know how to do so. Many are unable to build bridges between their students and the curriculum because they lack familiarity with communities their students come from, but then attribute students' reaction to an alienating curriculum as disinterest in learning.

Teachers can learn to teach diverse populations well, but doing so does not happen automatically. It is particularly difficult to get White preservice teachers to grapple substantively and constructively with race and ethnicity, and initiating such work can be very risky. In this book, Dr. Andrew Jackson, Sr. documents a process he used to prompt action in one university, to address this urgent need. Dr. Jackson has a long-standing track record of activism on behalf of students of color. He is well-known in the National Association for Multicultural Education, which was where I became acquainted with him.

In this book, Dr. Jackson uses the work of James Banks as a launch pad for curriculum reform in a school of education. It is particularly fitting that he should do so, since Banks (2006) has suggested that "The greatest promise of ethnic studies is that it will serve as a vehicle for general curriculum reform" (p. 70). Banks' work springs from a sustained, passionate conviction that humans are capable of constructing more humane societies than we have thus far, and that education is our most valuable resource for this purpose. Banks makes clear connections between intellectual and moral responsibilities of education. He challenges educators to prepare young people for participation in a diverse democracy in such a way that everyone sees her or his own fate tied to that of others, and no one has to leave his or her identity behind as a condition of participating. The vantage point of peoples who have been excluded, such as African Americans, prompts insights that tend to be absent when curriculum is constructed from the vantage point of power-holders.

Dr. Jackson traces many of the most significant themes in James Banks' work, connecting those to the work of other scholars in the area of multicultural education, in order to establish a base for curriculum reform. This book then presents a pilot course that makes use of the work of Banks and other multicultural education scholars, and it reports a study examining the need for reform of the undergraduate curriculum for teacher preparation.

Readers who seek to prompt their own universities to undertake a critical self-examination of the extent to which teachers are being prepared to teach diverse learners will benefit from the research and thinking that Dr. Jackson offers in this book. The challenge he raises is important. Schools of education cannot assume that preparation to teach "generic" students actually prepares teachers for students in classrooms today and tomorrow. Classrooms are transforming; teacher education must also be transformed. By grounding that transformation in the work of James Banks, Dr. Jackson recommends that we begin with roots of multicultural education and conceptual tools that are fundamental to the field.

Banks, J. A. (2006). *Race, culture, and education*. New York: Routledge.

Acknowledgments

I would like to gratefully acknowledge all of the faculty, staff, friends, and students who have contributed to this endeavor over the many years and stages of this research. I hope that all these combined efforts will add to the scholarship on multicultural education and that it will one day be embedded in the curriculum at all schools, colleges and universities. I would like to especially thank my committee members who shared with me their time and thinking to help me organize my thoughts and to bring this process to closure. Dr. Walter Terrell Jones, Dr. Edgar I. Farmer, Dr. James B. Stewart, Dr. Henry A. Giroux, Dr. David McBride, Dr. Daniel Walden, and Dr. Joseph J. Kockelmans worked at various stages of the study to see that it met all the criteria for good research, rigorous scholarship, and was approved by the Pennsylvania State University, Graduate School and the Office of Research Protections in 212 Kern Building, University Park, PA (www.

research.psu.edu/orp/)(814-865-1775), after meeting all of that office's guidelines and requirements. I would like to thank everyone who participated in the research assistance, proof-reading and editing process and technical support. Special thanks to Dr. Ronald Jackson II, Dr. Earnest Blackshear, Dr. Rodrick Stevenson, Burell Whitworth, Marcus Whitehurst, Wayne Gersie, Edward Thompson, Caleph Wilson, Ronel Smack, Greg Drane, Warren Hodge, Elaine Richardson for moral support and Cindi Fetters, Dorothy Thomas, Jill (Jellybean) Smith, and Lee Carpenter for proofreading and editing, Susan Wenger, Book Editor (very much appreciated for professional and technical assistance), Maurice Mosi McMorris for proofreading and editing, as well as all my peer editors who helped review my early drafts.

I would like to also thank my family--my very supportive and loving wife, Victoria Torres Jackson; daughters, Victoria Andrea and Mia Marie; and my son, Drew, Jr.,--for persevering with me throughout this arduous process. I dedicate this study to all the educators who join me in pursuing multicultural education, diversity awareness, and improving cross-cultural communications among all people. Special acknowledgment is attributed to the spiritual support from all my brothers (Dennis Maurice, Norman Jerome, Eric Leroy, Christopher Winfred, Antonio Pierre, the late Lucius, Jr., Floyd, Lewis, Ira Lee (Dulah), and the late Thomas Lee and my sisters Amanda and the late Rebecca, for their love and support passed down by my late parents, Lucius and Essie Mae (Clements) Jackson, and all my relatives and friends who have supported me throughout my formal educational endeavors. This project started conceptually after my graduation from the Penn State University in the College of Education in 1974, and my return to Penn State University 12 years later, in 1986, after teaching in Elverson Elementary School in District 5, North Philadelphia, Tasker Elementary School in District 2, South Philadelphia in the Philadelphia School District in Philadelphia, Pa, Southeast Delco School District in Folcroft, Pa at Ashland Middle School and Academy Park High School, Chester Upland School District in Chester, Pa, at Smedley Middle School and the Interim Learning Center at Chester High School, Widener University, as a counselor in the Act 101 and Star Honors Program, Temple University in the Career Development and Placement Center and the Mid Atlantic Network of National Teacher Corps, and my return experiences at Penn State in the College of Education Office of Teacher Certification Services and Recruitment for the past 20 years. I hope to continue teaching, advising, service, community service, and research in the field of multicultural education and diversity training, as I conclude my 4th year (1999-2003) as Past President of the Pennsylvania Chapter of the National Association for Multicultural Education and begin my first term as the NAME Region #3 Director (2003-2005) (for Pennsylvania, Maryland, West Virginia, Virginia, Washington, DC, and Delaware), with the NAME Office located at 5272 River RD, Suite 430, Bethesda, Maryland 20816 (301-951-0022) (fax: 301-951-0023).(www.nameorg. org) and (wvvw.ed.psu.edu/multicultural-ed).

CHAPTER 1

Introduction

Historical Perspectives

A goal of the *Framework to Foster Diversity at Penn State: 1998-2003* (Penn State University, 2003, p. 1) is to institute curricular and research initiatives that provide students with the skills and orientation to function effectively in multicultural workplaces and social environments. "This perspective has led many colleges and universities to mandate that students complete courses addressing diversity subject matter in order to graduate. One objective of such a requirement is the cultivation of cross-cultural communication and interaction skills," according to this writer.

An individual who has been influential in the theory of multicultural education over the past 30 years is James A. Banks. His work has been instrumental in sharing teaching strategies for multicultural education among many educators and theorists on multicultural education and diversity issues. His commitment to connecting education to a multicultural context is clear in his comment that:

> Education within a pluralistic society should affirm and help students understand their home and community cultures. However, it should also help free them from their cultural boundaries. To create and maintain a civic community that works for the common good, education in a democratic society should help students acquire the knowledge, attitudes, and skills they will need to participate in civic action to make society more equitable and just (Banks, 1995).

Purpose

The purpose of this study is to introduce, support and validate the need for a multicultural education and diversity course in Colleges of Education based on the framework and the works of James A. Banks, Director of the Center for the Study of Multicultural Education at the University of Washington in Seattle, and other multicultural education theorists. The strategic plan in the Penn State College of Education (1998-2003) supports the need for more course diversity surrounding issues of race, sexual orientation issues, gay, lesbian, bi-sexual, trans-gender, religion, ethnicity, and equity issues.

One goal and focus of this study was to examine the work of James A. Banks in the evolution of multicultural education using the mechanism of a specially designed summer 2001 pilot course in the Penn State College of Education and a survey research instrument designed by the researcher to collect data for further analysis in the study. In addition, this study examines teacher education strategies and suggestions for developing curriculum in multicultural education, and particularly in the social justice concerns of equity in education. It is this researcher's belief that more course offerings should be made available to share multicultural education concepts with faculty, staff, and students in College of Education teacher training programs as well as throughout the University. A pilot research course was developed during the summer 2001 session at Penn State to field test Banks' strategies for curricular reform with students and community participants. A multicultural research survey was administered to four groups of 25 students in Curriculum and Instruction (CI 495) with support from faculty and instructors at Penn State in Language and Literacy classes (LLED 411 and 412), Clinical Field Experience classes, Early Child Hood Education classes (ECE 451 and 452), and Psychology 002 classes.

The additional data collected for the survey instrument were collected and the survey instrument and study were approved by Penn State's Office of Research Protections. The data were collected and the following variables were added: race, ethnicity, and gender, number of diversity courses taken, and year in school.

Multicultural education has increased significantly in our nation, primarily because of the interest of education leaders in diversity and climate issues. Although many conceptions of multicultural education now exist, the work of James A. Banks stands out as one of the earliest and succinct approaches. His theories continue to serve as the foundation for contemporary dialogues about multicultural education. Although Banks' work occupies a privileged position in the history of the development of multicultural education, there have been remarkably few studies that report the results of efforts to implement his theories in training prospective teachers. Responding to this deficit, this pilot study provides useful information about the potential benefits and challenges associated with implementing Banks' multicultural education theories in a teacher education curriculum. The approach to implementing Banks' theories undertaken in this pilot study can also be applied to other approaches to multicultural education that use different classification schemes and propose different emphases.

This study examines specific teacher education recommendations for curriculum development with the central focus on multicultural education as viewed in works by Banks. The work by Banks and other multicultural educators such as Christine Sleeter (1989, 1994), Carl A. Grant (1988, 1995), Asa Hilliard III (1990), Donna Gollnick (1990, 1999), Philip Chinn (1990, 1999), Sonia Nieto (1999, 2000), Carlos Cortes, (1973/1995, 2002), Geneva Gay (1995), and John Ogbu (1988) has built on historical efforts to reform education and responds to changing racial, religious, ethnic, and changing demography. This study also provides a comparative perspective, but focuses on specific teacher education recommendations for developing curriculum.

The educational reform movement has its roots in the societal and historical forces that started after World War I and following the period as the Americanization and Nativism Movements (Takaki, 1995). The Americanization period was the period devoted to making immigrants become more like Americans by surrendering their native language in order to learn English and in some cases changing the pronunciation and spelling of their last name or first name to sound more American.

The Nativism movement was the period that forced new immigrants from Europe to adapt to becoming new Americans in the United States or suffer rejection, ostracism or isolation from the more senior or long-term immigrants (Schlesinger, 1995). Mass immigration occurred before World War II, and the field-to-factory migration of African Americans from the South to the North occurred from the 1920s to the 1940s, during the Great Migration.

The current significant and high rates of immigration to the U.S. from Asia, Africa, Europe, North and South America, the Caribbean, and other parts of the world contribute to new forms of racism and prejudice. Despite the struggle to develop multicultural education, there are vigorous indications of the formalization of multicultural education. Authors from a variety of disciplines and perspectives have begun to formulate the philosophical and theoretical under-pinnings of multicultural education (Banks, 1994; Bennett, 1995;Colangelo, Dustin & Foxley, 1985; Gollnick & Chinn, 1986; Grant, 1995; Grant & Sleeter, 1988; Nieto, 1992).

Multicultural education attempts to combat social dynamics fostering racism and prejudice by preparing teachers to address issues of cross-cultural contact in a classroom setting. Even though there are debates about the nature of multiculturalism, there is reasonable consensus that the issue of preparing students to live harmoniously in an increasingly diverse society is important (Banks, 1997). This researcher believes that a variety of innovative approaches to the education of young students are being developed that requires more systematic teacher training strategies, like those formulated by Banks. We need different teaching strategies for the new millennium.

Curriculum issues such as classroom management and multicultural education are still not required in all pre-service teacher training programs. There is still no agreeable way to include multicultural education content in an appropriate and uniform way across teacher training programs (Banks, 1997). Every educator should know their own cultural identity and should be able to recognize biases and prejudices, which can be addressed in a non-threatening manner with different educational strategies over time. Educators need to learn about different cultural groups other than their own. The ultimate goal of multicultural education is to meet the individual learning needs of each student so that all students can progress to the fullest capacity. This goal has not been reached in the past because educators have been unable to use effectively the cultural backgrounds of students in providing classroom instruction (Gollnick & Chinn, 1990).

Significance of the Study

James Banks' approach to multicultural education represents one of many schools of thought. In Banks' view, education within a pluralistic society should affirm and help students understand their home and community cultures (Banks, 1997). Multicultural education should help free students from their cultural boundaries and to create and maintain a civic community. Multicultural education should promote strategies in education, which helps to create models of curriculum design that works for the common good.

Multicultural education has become a popular concept in many educational institutions, in part because the concept enabled schools, colleges, and universities to pool limited resources and thus to focus on a wide range of groups rather than to address the concerns of each group individually (Banks & Banks, 1993).

Although the NCATE standards have promoted multicultural education in school curricula, State Departments of Education have still not made it mandatory for certification in teacher education programs across the country. The NCATE (1977, 1979, 2000, 2001) diversity standards were first published as part of the Council's general standards in

1977 and have been revised and re-issued through the years. NCATE is now developing performance-based standards with implications for diversity enhancement in the curriculum. In 1979, NCATE included multicultural education amongst its criteria for accreditation of teacher preparation programs. Many colleges and universities still have not included multicultural education in their requirements for certification or licensure. Multicultural education is currently an integral part of diversity standards for NCATE (1999, 2000) in 25 of 50 states.

Each of us has many aspects to our selves, race, gender, age, class, religion, sexual orientation, language, ability, etc. The different ways in which multicultural education has been conceptualized has resulted in different models for designing curriculum and instructional material. People function as individuals, as members of sub- groups, and as citizens in a common democracy (Haddad, 1995).

Earlier responses of schools to address inequality, curriculum inclusion, and curriculum reform to eliminate and address issues such as prejudice and racism, involved combinations of ethnic studies research on curricular reform with an emphasis on prejudice reduction inherited from both the ethnic studies movement and the inter-group education movement.

Ethnic content was quickly incorporated in textbooks, sometimes as superficially as coloring White faces brown in a few illustrations (Sleeter & Grant, 1991). Curriculum units focused on different ethnic groups and ethnic holidays were celebrated in schools. These reforms were often called multi-ethnic education, rather than multicultural education, since their primary focus was on ethnic groups (Banks, 1973c, 1973d, 1975a).

Multicultural education was originally defined primarily in terms of racial/ethnic minority groups whose academic achievement levels were below those of the European American majority. Its scope expanded to embrace a variety of other victimized groups: women, speakers of other languages other than English, the poor, the handicapped, the disabled, LGBT, the aged, and other special interest groups. Race, class, gender, cognitive styles, and language are the variables most often addressed, vastly differing emphases and interpretations. Some of Banks' major concerns in addressing curriculum reform included an understanding and awareness of these issues:

1. Content integration, which deals with the extent to which teachers use examples and content from a variety of cultures and groups to illustrate key concepts, generalizations, and issues within their subject areas or disciplines.

2. Knowledge construction, which is a process that describes how the biases, frames of reference, and perspectives within a discipline influence the ways in which knowledge is constructed within it (Banks, 1996).

3. Prejudice reduction, which describes lessons and activities used by teachers to help students to develop positive attitudes toward different racial, ethnic, and cultural groups. Research indicates also that lessons, units, and teaching materials include content about different racial and ethnic groups. These kinds of activities can help students to develop more positive personal self-identity and inter-group attitudes if certain conditions exist in the curriculum to reinforce self-identity (Banks, 1995b).

4. Equity pedagogy, which exists according to Banks when teachers modify their teaching in ways that will facilitate the academic achievement of students from diverse racial, cultural, and social class groups (Banks & Banks, 1993).

5. Building and empowering school climate, social structure, and culture are included in the social action and decision-making stage of multicultural education and development (Banks, 1995a.).

The thesis looked at the following questions as a starting point for developing the summer pilot research course and for determining the positive models for Banks as a pioneer in multicultural education and curriculum reform models.

Research Questions

1. What are the implications of Banks' models for multicultural education in the design of a multicultural course for teachers in a College of Education?

2. What are the relative strengths and weaknesses of Banks' teacher training recommendations compared to those of other prominent multicultural education theorists?

3. Can a multicultural education course using Banks be designed and delivered during a summer session, in which students transition through Banks' stages of understanding?

4. To what extent does Banks' approach to multicultural education provide concrete guidelines for teacher training?

The concept of multicultural education evolved and took shape in the United States out of the social turmoil in the United States in the late 1960s, throughout the 1970s, into the 1980s during the Reagan era, and into the present era. The linkages between diverse and coexisting ethnic, racial, socioeconomic heritages have been explored. There has been very enthusiastic support for the promotion of multicultural education and diversity in the curriculum. When the first courses in multicultural education were developed in the 1960s, the United States was in the midst of urban and social crises, and few textbooks were available on this literature.

Limitations of the Study

The main limitation was the short time interval for setting up the 6-week summer pilot course and the short time frame for recruiting more students during the summer session as opposed to the 15-week time available for fall or spring semester Another limitation was the focus on College of Education undergraduates, as well as a small sample of students and a not large enough sample of Asian, African American and Hispanic students in the target population. The limitations are that Single Group Studies focus primarily on one group (College of Education, Penn State students) and do not necessarily promote the inclusion of all groups (other colleges) in that particular design.

Key Definitions

Multicultural Education Models and Curriculum Reform

Anti-bias—An active/activist approach to challenging prejudice, stereotyping, bias, and the "isms" in a society in which institutional structures create and maintain sexism, racism, and (disabled).

Bias—Any attitude, belief, or feeling that results in, and

helps to justify, unfair treatment of an individual because of his identity.

Census—A periodic governmental enumeration of population; takes place every ten years for congressional reapportioning and other information gathering purposes

Classism—A term used to describe preferential treatment as a result of socio- economic status or position.

Content Integration—Teaching information from various cultures in the curriculum.

Cultural assimilation—Takes place when one ethnic or cultural group acquires the behavior, values, perspectives, ethos, and characteristics of another ethnic group and sheds its own cultural characteristics.

Cultural Diversity—The condition of many different traditions and cultures within a larger society.

Cultural Shock—Finding oneself all alone in a new environment (country, language, food, music, etc.) with different cultural traits and customs.

Disabilities or Disabled—A description of persons with a condition perceived as a handicap. Institutional practices prevent the integration of disabled people into the mainstream of society and keep them socially and economically oppressed.

Discrimination—The differential treatment of individuals or groups based on categories such as race, ethnicity, gender, sexual orientation, social class, or exceptionality.

Empowering School Climate and Community—Allowing

citizens the opportunity for making a difference and breaking down barriers and stereotypes

Equity Pedagogy—Explores techniques to assist low achieving students to attain greater academic achievement.

Ethnic Group—A micro-cultural group or collectivity that shares a common history and culture, common values, behaviors, and other characteristics that cause members of the group to have a shared identity. A sense of people hood is one of the most important characteristics of an ethnic group. An ethnic group- also shares economic and political interests. Cultural characteristics rather than biological traits, are the essential attributes of an ethnic group. An ethnic group is not the same as a racial group

Homo-phobia—A fear and hatred of gay men and lesbian women backed up by institutional policies and power that discriminates against them.

Knowledge Construction—The process of developing knowledge bases for curriculum integration, infusion, and understanding.

People of Color—All the different national or ethnic groups that are targets of racism in the United States.

Prejudice—An attitude, opinion, or feeling formed without adequate prior knowledge, thought, or reason.

Pre-prejudice—Beginning ideas and feelings in very young children that may develop into real prejudice through reinforcement by prevailing societal biases.

Prejudice Reduction—The process of reducing prejudice in society.

Racism—Any attitude, action, or institutional practice backed up by institutional power that subordinates people because of their skin color

Sexism—Any attitude, action, or institutional power that subordinates people because of their sex.

Stereotype—An oversimplified generalization about a particular group, race, sex, which carries derogatory implications.

Whites—All the different national ethnic groups of European origin who as a group are disproportionately represented in the control of the economic, political, and cultural institutions in the United States

Banks' Four Curriculum Reform Approaches

Additive Approach—When content, concepts, themes, and perspectives are added to the curriculum without changing its structure.

Ethnic Contributions—Approach focuses on heroes, holidays, and discrete cultural elements in the school curriculum.

Transformative Approach—When the structure of the curriculum is changed to enable students to view concepts, issues, events, and themes from the perspective of diverse ethnic and cultural groups.

Social Action and Decision Making Approach—When students make decisions on important social issues and take actions to help solve them.

Organization of the Study

Chapter 2 reviews the relevant literature in the study of multicultural education and introduces the ideas of James A. Banks, beginning with his Ph.D. study in 1969, "A Content Analysis of elementary American History Textbooks: The Treatment of the Negro and Race Relations", Michigan State University, Department of Elementary and special Education, College of Education and an article in Social Education, December 1969, in addition to his work on Black Self-Identity in the early 1970s.

Chapter 3 presents research design and methodology, the survey research instrument and the design for the analysis and evaluation of the pilot course, which includes a review of Banks' models for curriculum reform focusing on the ethnic contributions approach, the additive content curriculum reform approach, the transformative approach, and the decision making and social action approach to curriculum reform. These models were used in interpreting the curriculum guidelines and curriculum reform and inclusion frameworks used by Banks. The thesis looked at several approaches by Banks, such as the additive approach, contributions approach, transformation approach, and social action and decision-making curriculum reform approach. The study also reviewed models similar to those by Banks, such as the work by Christine Sleeter and Carl A. Grant (1988, 1995), on the race, class, gender, ethnicity, and social action and decision-making approach to curriculum reform and integration supported by Banks as well.

Chapter 4 interprets the survey research findings and analyzes the data, reflections, and evaluations from the pilot course and the survey findings.

Chapter 5 gives suggestions and recommendations for incorporating multicultural education into the curriculum with an interdisciplinary focus.

CHAPTER 2

Literature Review

This chapter provides an overview of James Banks' work in the general field of education and more specifically in multicultural education. The chapter is organized according to the following themes: (1) The influence of Banks' theories on multicultural education; (2) Banks' influence on the social sciences; (3) Banks and identity development; (4) the evolution of the concept of multicultural education; (5) Banks' major contributions to the multicultural education dialogue; (6) Banks and multicultural curriculum reform; (7) the influence of Banks' theories on other multicultural educators and curricula; and (8) critics of multiculturalism.

This chapter also synthesizes the writings of Banks and other authors on the subject of multicultural education, focusing on Banks' contributions to the subject of multicultural education. Multicultural teaching begins with the realization that the teacher plays a major role in empowering or dis-empowering students in the classroom. A multicultural teacher begins the education process of self-education by examining his or her values, beliefs, and visions of life, including prejudices and discomfort with certain issues. Other supportive people in the teaching process include co-teachers, guest speakers, teaching assistants, and other students. The key in developing the ideal multicultural environment is to create and foster a diverse teaching team that collaborates well. Another key quality is knowledge of multicultural education as it has evolved in U.S. education institutions. This knowledge would include familiarity with the work of James Banks.

Banks is credited (Haddad, 1995) with being the grandfather of multicultural education for his contributions to the discipline over the past 30 years, particularly to the theory and practice of multiculturalism and curriculum pedagogy. James Banks was born in Mariana, Arkansas in 1941. He graduated from Chicago City College with an Associate of Arts degree in 1963, and from Chicago State University with a Bachelor of Education degree in 1964. After completing his bachelor's degree, Banks taught in Joliet, Illinois. He published several articles while teaching at Francis W. Parker School in Chicago, Illinois, before completing his first major project while pursuing his Master's and Doctoral Degrees in Education and Social Sciences at Michigan State University. One of Dr. Banks' first major research and scholarship projects was his Master's project on "Teacher Attitudes and Expectations of Socially Disadvantaged Youths", at Michigan

State University in March 1967, which was summarized in the March 1967 issue of *Phi Delta Kappan* magazine.

Banks wrote about teaching, writing, reading, the arts, and social studies in the late 1960s before focusing on multi-ethnic and multi-cultural educational strategies for teachers. He wrote that teachers in the inner city were most dissatisfied with discipline and classroom behavior that affects student learning outcomes and time on task in class. Strategies needed to be considered and developed for addressing the behaviors of ethnic students, particularly those in the public schools. This subject was the focus of his article, "Why Teachers are Dissatisfied" (Banks, 1967a). He also wrote about "Art in the Social Studies" (Banks, 1967b) and "Searching for the Unknown in Fractions" (Banks, 1967c), which focused on content material appropriate for elementary students. His most impressive work was his doctoral study, "A Content Analysis of Elementary History Textbooks: The Treatment of the Negro and Race Relations," completed in 1969. Banks' other early contributions include, "A Content Analysis of the Black American in Text books" (Banks, 1969), "The Need for Positive Racial Attitudes in Textbooks" (Banks, 1969a), "Relevant Social Studies for Black Pupils" (Banks, 1969b), "Developing Racial Tolerance with Literature on the Black Inner City" (Banks, 1970a), "Teaching the Black Experience: Methods and Materials" (Banks, 1970b), and "March Toward Freedom: A History of Black Americans" (Banks, 1974). The latter set of articles displays his feelings about African Americans' contributions to U.S. society and emerge from his earlier ideas about curriculum before he began his examination of the concept of a multicultural curriculum.

The Influence of Banks' Theories on Multicultural Education

The term multicultural is in itself problematic, encompassing a whole range of differing interpretations. What do we mean by multicultural teaching? How do we understand, confront, and relate the various sources of cultural differentiation such as race, gender, class, sexual orientation, ethnicity, and religion? These are the growing concerns of all educators in schools and colleges today, and highlight some of the questions for which educators seek answers as they design curricula on multicultural education. Fortunately, guidance is available in a significant literature, much of which has either been written by or influenced by Banks.

Banks' influence on education theories stems from his development of research and theories on curriculum reform over the past 30 years. Some of this work occurred during his employment as a third-, fourth-, and fifth-grade teacher; other elements arose from his work on black positive self-identity as exhibited in textbook narratives, uncovered during his research for his study. Furthermore, Banks' study shaped his interest in and thoughts on multicultural education as an academic studies discipline in the early 1970s and on multiethnic and multiracial curriculum integration and school reform in the school curriculum.

Banks' major contributions to multicultural education are his development of theory and his evaluation of the research literatures on several related themes. His considerable academic reputation reflects the depth and breadth of his scholarship and his ability to recognize and incorporate into his work the concerns and philosophical loyalties of a broad constituency of people (Haddad, 1995).

In Banks' "knowledge construction process," the focus is on the language arts curriculum, pedagogy, and the "the manner in which the implicit assumptions, frames of reference, perspectives, and biases within a discipline influence the ways that knowledge is constructed within it" (Banks, 1995, p. 4). No knowledge is neutral: rather, "the positions of both the Western traditionalists and the multiculturalists reflect values, ideologies, political positions, and human interests" (Banks, 1996a, p. 5). The knowledge of teachers is socially, historically, and philosophically constructed, and that realization makes a critical examination possible. Banks (1996a) promotes this critical approach by defining transformative academic knowledge as" the facts, concepts, paradigms, themes, and explanations that challenge mainstream academic knowledge and expand and substantially revise established canons, paradigms, theories, explanations, and research methods" (1996a, p. 9). What teachers teach and what students learn is based on the types of knowledge and how knowledge is valued, and how and why it is constructed.

Banks (1993c) discerned four phases in the emergence of multicultural education since the early 1970s. According to Banks, ethnic studies constitute the first phase which deals with understanding and analyzing ethnic groups in America and around the world such as Hispanics/Latinos, East Asians, Native Americans, European and Middle Easterners, North, South, and Central Americans, and other groups around the world. The second phase involves a call for general school reform to increase educational equality in schools in America to create educational equity in institutions and organizations. The third phase has to do with the incorporation of the concerns of other groups, such as women and people with disabilities as well as gay, lesbian, bi-sexual, and trans-gendered persons who may feel discriminated against in society. The fourth phase focuses on the development of theory and practice related to the interrelation of the variables of race, class, ethnicity, religion, diversity, ageism, and gender issues. Multicultural education, according to Banks, is multi-faceted, with at least three different manifestations: (1) as an idea or concept; (2) as an educational reform movement; and (3) as a process (Banks, 1989b).

By the late 1970s, Banks had moved from concern with ethnic minorities to concern for all students. By the 1980s, Banks viewed school reform as essential not only to helping students develop cross-cultural competence, but also to giving all students an equal opportunity to learn (Banks, 1989b).

Banks' interest in race, religion, sexual orientation, ethnicity, diversity, class, and gender issues influenced his framework for multi-racial, multiethnic, and multicultural education. His early interest in race and equal opportunity for advancement in education and jobs, and curriculum inclusion began in the 1960s. According to Banks (1991a), developing and teaching a multicultural curriculum that focuses on powerful concepts and ideas requires an understanding of knowledge categories and their relationships: facts, concepts, and generalizations (Banks, 1991 a). Facts are low-level, specific empirical statements. Concepts are words or phrases that enable people to categorize or classify a large class of observations to reduce the complexity of their world. Generalizations are tested or verified statements that contain two or more concepts and explanations for their relationship.

Throughout his career, Banks has identified areas of content integration upon which teachers need to improve, such as curriculum design, inclusion, and a better awareness and understanding of multicultural issues that affect all people. Knowledge construction helps teachers to understand the different perspectives of students (Banks, 1996) and the process and different states of awareness and understanding of different racial and ethnic identities for Whites, Blacks, Asians, and Native Americans, and those experiencing other racial identities and transformations.

Developing approaches to multicultural curriculum reform is one of Banks' major contributions. These approaches include: The Contributions Approach, Level 1, focuses on heroes, holidays, and discrete cultural elements such as Cinco de Mayo (May 5th). Cinco de Mayo is celebrated by

Mexicans and Hispanics, while Asian Pacific Month, Puerto Rican Heritage Month, Black History Month, Women's History Month, etc., are other recognized cultural events and holidays.

Level 2, the Additive Approach, has to do with those occasions when content, concepts, themes, and perspectives are added to the curriculum without changing its structure. The additive approach is often accomplished by the addition of a book, unit, or a specific course to the curriculum. The Transformation Approach, Level 3, involves changing the structure of the curriculum to enable students to view concepts, issues, events, and themes from the perspective of diverse ethnic and cultural groups. Level 4, the Social Action Approach, is when students make decisions on important social issues and take actions to help solve them.

Banks identified activities engaged in by teachers to help students develop positive attitudes toward different racial, ethnic, and cultural groups in society (Banks, 1995b). Some of these activities are embedded in the four curriculum reform areas of additive identity, ethnic contributions, transformative curriculum reform, and decision making, and social action activities in the curriculum. The goal of gathering such information is to further Equity Pedagogy by teachers, to facilitate academic achievement by all groups, and to build an empowering school climate in decision-making and social action (Banks, 1995a). When Banks first wrote about multicultural education in the 1970s (Banks, 1976), he described his work as multiethnic education at that time (Banks,

1977b, 1977d). He preferred the narrower focus of multiethnic studies because he recognized that multicultural implies a more inclusive association with People of Color. Ethnicity is a complex concept (Banks, 1975a, 1978a, 1981 c) that includes an individual's psychological identity with his or her ethnic group (Banks, 1980, p. 118). Banks conceptualized ethnic group membership across a number of variables that exist on a continuum that includes language, non-verbal communications, world-views, values, epistemology, and ethnic identification (Banks, 1980, 1981b).

In his work Banks captured an essential element of American citizenship that is missing in much of the literature on citizenship education: questions and issues related to race, ethnicity, and social-class stratification. The thousands of immigrants who enter the United States each year, the increasing number of students who speak a first language other than English, and the widening gap between the rich and the poor intensify the challenge of educating students for citizenship in a democratic society. Banks described how schools can both educate students to participate effectively in a society that reflects ethnic and cultural diversity and promote national unity and public good. He described in his works how the concepts, paradigms, and aims of multicultural education must become integral parts of citizenship education to create democratic free-thinking schools.

More specific examples of the adaptation of curricula to better address the needs of diverse student populations can be found in the work of Grant and Sleeter (1998), Davidman and Davidman (1994, 1997, 2001), and "Multicultural Perspectives: A Practical Guide to Multicultural Education" and "Multicultural Learning Activities" (Tiedt & Tiedt, 1999, 2000, 2001).

Banks' Influence on the Social Sciences

During the 1960s and 1970s, many African American scholars (John Hope Franklin, Geneva Gay, Lerone Bennett, author of "Before the Mayflower: A History of Black America," "The Shaping of Black America: The Struggles and Triumphs of African Americans, 1619 to the 1990s" reprinted (1969, 1970, 1971, 1972, 1973, 1974, 1975), including Banks, challenged traditional interpretations of African American slavery, the African American family, and Black English that had been made by non- African social scientists and had become institutionalized in the social science literature and in the curriculum of schools and universities. Overturning these interpretations was necessary for many reasons, not the least of which was their influence on educational theories and practices, and on public policy.

The most noted example of the influence of social science research on public policy during the 1950s and 1960s was the Civil Rights legislation that emerged after *Brown v. Board of Education* (1954), which highlighted the social, economic, and political discrimination experienced by African Americans in America and called for a redress of these social injustices. Banks noted that social science research that supported equity issues for African Americans in particular and other racial groups more generally became highly visible and was influential in shaping public policy (Banks, 1997). The court ruled in the *Brown v. Board of Education* case (1954) that segregated educational facilities are "inherently unequal because of the psychological harm they cause African American children and youths" (*Brown v. Board of Education*) (Davidman & Davidman, 2001, p. 93).

Chief Justice Warren, for the court, wrote, "To separate African American children from others of similar age and qualifications solely because of race generates a feeling of inferiority as to their status in the community that may affect their hearts and minds in a way unlikely to ever be undone" (*Brown v. Board of Education,* 1954). Expanded rights for students with disabilities were one of the major consequences of the Civil Rights Movement of the 1960s and 1970s (Grant, 1995). The Supreme Court's Brown decision, issued in 1954, established the principle that to segregate students solely because of their race is inherently unequal and unconstitutional. This decision, as well as other legal and social reforms of the 1960s, encouraged advocates for the rights of students with disabilities to push for expanded rights (Grant, 1995). If it were unconstitutional to segregate students because of their race, it was reasoned, segregating students because they were disabled could also be challenged. It must be understood in the literature that disabilities were highlighted as part of the struggle for addressing curriculum reform and access to education.

Advocates for the rights of students with disabilities experienced a major victory in 1975 when Congress enacted Public Law 94-142, The Education for All Handicapped Children Act. The controversy over gifted education stems in part from the belief by many people that it is elitist. Other educators may argue that gifted education is a way for powerful mainstream parents to acquire a special education for their children in the public schools. The fact that few students of color are classified as gifted is another source of controversy. Disabled students are being discussed here as a part of the disenfranchised population of minorities that curriculum reform was trying to address.

Banks and Identity Development

In the last several decades, individuals have been responding more actively to political and personal pressures to identify with a specific group that shares their cultural background. For the growing number of individuals of mixed racial, ethnic, and cultural heritage living in the U.S., deciding to make such an identification is complicated, and sometimes problematic, although families ease this process for their children by teaching about race and ethnicity from their perspective and ancestry (Root, 1992).

Now, with more than 100,000 multiracial babies, representing a wide variety of ethnic mixes, being born annually (Grant & Ladson-Billings, 1995), it is also important for society in general to foster the positive development of these individuals by respecting and appreciating their distinctness.

Most research on identity development claims that an individual will need to have a clarified identity before being able to recognize or address societal change (Banks, 1994). Banks focused on the Positive Self Identity of African American children in his early works in the late 1960s before moving on to a more inclusive focus on all people of color in the early 1970s.

The dimensions of multicultural education developed by Banks (1995a) provide the conceptual framework for the development of his concepts of content integration, knowledge construction process, prejudice reduction, equity pedagogy, and an empowering school culture and social structure. Banks acknowledges that to implement multicultural education effectively, teachers and administrators must attend to each of the five dimensions of multicultural education mentioned above. An important goal in multicultural education has been to improve race relations through the school curriculum and the empowerment of students through knowledge and curriculum content.

In *Multicultural Education, Transformative Knowledge, and Action* (Banks, 1996b), Banks focuses on knowledge construction and social action as well as the concept of prejudice reduction. Scholarship on race, sex, gender, ethnicity and diversity issues should be included in the pre-service training for teachers to develop a broader awareness of all students.

Examples of this scholarship include Ronald Takaki's thoughtful and informative book, *A Different Mirror: A History of Multicultural America* (1993); Gloria Anzaldua's,

Borderlands/La Frontera (1987); Gary Y. Okihiro's, *Margins and Mainstreams: Asians in American History and Culture* (1994).

Transformative scholarship may be used to transform the school, college, and university curriculum. Special efforts need to be made by teachers to include works that deal with women of color, such as those by Carby (1992) and hooks (1984). Scholarship by men of color often has been as silent on women's issues as that by White men (hooks & West, 1991). Transformative scholarship on women of color is rich in insights and concepts. Important works include *Black Women in America: A Historical Encyclopedia*, edited by Darlene Clark Hine (1993). With this literature and framework in place for curriculum development and revision, educational curricula may evolve into more socially representative, or multicultural, curricula.

Banks believes that cultural identities are developed according to the types of literature available in the curriculum (Banks, 1994, 1995). Multicultural literature explores the race and ethnicity of others. Some strategies used by multiculturalists include instructional strategies that foster an effective as well as an intellectual identification with literary characters through strategies of reader response. This is called biblio-therapy.

Such strategies may include asking students to re-experience their literary response by acting it out or retelling evocative events, imagining or picturing characters or settings of events from the selection; applying personal experiences;

applying other readers or media to the work; applying other readers views to examine their own responses; re-examining the text from other perspectives; and reflecting upon or generalizing the meaning of the literary experience. Biblio-therapy may be used for personal assessment and growth. It draws upon psychoanalytic theory to hypothesize a therapeutic effect of identification, catharsis, and insight through reading. Ethno-biblio- therapy is a term used by Geneva Gay (1985) to describe an instructional technique that uses literature written from an experiential, personal point of view (novels, short stories, autobiographies, and plays) to help students learn ways of coping with different ethnic dilemmas.

An individual's sense of self with respect to their membership in and feelings of identification with a distinct cultural group with whom they share certain phenotypic and cultural characteristics, such as language, religion, and customs, helps distinguish racial and ethnic identity from other members in society. Multicultural education is an approach to teaching and learning that is based upon democratic values and beliefs and seeks to foster cultural pluralism with culturally diverse societies (Banks, 1994, p. 4).

Banks (1994b, p. 4) noted that despite attempts made in schools to apply multicultural education to the curriculum, many schools and university practitioners have a limited conception of multicultural education and view it primarily as curriculum reform that involves changing or restructuring the curriculum to include content about ethnic groups, women, and other cultural groups.

The Evolution of the Concept of Multicultural Education

Banks (1993e) expressed the hope that multicultural education is now developing a status as an academic discipline in its own right, much like sociology and anthropology. The traditional approach in the academy is to separate practice from knowing. In the most common case, the faculty member conducts research and teaches in the area of race relations but is not necessarily sensitive to students from different backgrounds. The university in the past may have made an institutional commitment to recruit faculty from historically underrepresented groups but insufficient support has been provided to construct and foster a truly multicultural institution in terms of culture, values, and ideology.

A university may hire new faculty and admit students from underrepresented groups, but the traditional dominant group remains in power. There is no change in the curriculum or reward structure and the budget and campus culture remain the same. These are some of the reasons and arguments for the evolution of multicultural education, which has emerged as a starting point for curriculum inclusion and organizational structural change.

Multiculturalism is inclusive of groups according to race, ethnicity, culture, gender, sexual orientation, religion, and socioeconomic class. The pilot course that was the focus of this study (described in chapters 3 and 4) was designed to validate a model for designing a multicultural method for inclusion and curriculum reform. The literature on multicultural education generally divides itself into three theoretical frameworks: conservative, liberal, and critical (McLaren & Giroux, 1994). Grant and Sleeter (1995) provided the label culturally different for the conservative approach to multiculturalism. Social mobility leading to equality comes from assimilation that requires the elimination of certain differences or deficits in knowledge, skills, and values that are barriers to the acquisition of better paying jobs. The teacher's job is to bridge the gaps between mainstream culture and the "culturally different" through remedial education that inculcates mainstream know-how.

Lisa Delpit, author of *Other Peoples Children* (1995), is among those who rejected the conservative agenda as one that ignores the effects on minorities of the "culture of power" and who argue against any action that negates children's knowledge of their culture and heritage. Delpit believed minority students must have access to the "codes of power" to be successful in school. Students must make it through the gate

keeping points by knowing standard English and code shifting from standard English to the vernacular when and if appropriate among peers.

Those who espouse critical multiculturalism believe that issues of equity and excellence cannot be addressed effectively without posing difficult but essential questions: Under what conditions and by whom are concepts of equity and excellence constructed? Banks asked, who is included under E

Pluribus Unum? Can all groups benefit equally from a particular construction of concepts? How can equity and excellence be achieved in a society in which historically the dominant culture has been determining their meaning and defining the meaning of others outside the dominant culture as well? Knowledge is not value free but shaped culturally, historically, ethnically, and linguistically. In Henry Giroux's words, knowledge "never speaks for itself, but rather is constantly mediated through the ideological and cultural experiences that students bring to the classroom" (Giroux, 1988, p. 100).

Grant and Sleeter described a liberal human relations approach to multi- culturalism for schools that attempts to promote acceptance of diversity through inter- group education based on the sharing of feelings and values. They pointed out that this liberal approach includes a limited analysis of why inequalities exist. An approach focused on "let's get to know each other" sidesteps the root causes of racism and inequality.

The social reconstructionist approach is the most visionary and critical of Grant and Sleeter's models. It directly challenges students to become social reformers and commit to the reconstruction of society through the redistribution of power and resources. The curriculum teaches social skills, promotes cultural pluralism and alternative life styles, and has students analyze oppression with the intent of eventually taking action as in Banks' Social Action and Decision-Making Approach to curriculum reform (Banks, 1994). The multicultural curriculum and pedagogy models by Banks (contributions model, additive model, transformative model, and social action model) are extremely important and demonstrate how elements of all three frameworks can work both alone and in combination to move schools toward a curriculum characterized by equity and excellence. Banks' models complement the models of Sleeter and Grant.

Banks wrote about African American experiences before including other groups in his work, such as Native Americans, Hispanics, Asians, and European Whites. His first book, *A March Toward Freedom: A History of Black Americans* (1970, 1974), traced the history of Blacks in America from the early days of slavery to the present in America.

Banks originally focused on the contributions of African Americans and ethnic contributions in history and social studies in the early 1970s. He later included all ethnic groups in his theory for curriculum reform and ethnic contributions in society. Banks' departure from an African American focus to a more multiethnic and multi-racial approach was due to resistance in the field to a single-group focus on educational and curricular issues (Haddad, 1995).

Banks' Major Contributions to the Multicultural Education Dialogue

Education equality for all students is unattainable without the incorporation of cultural pluralism in all aspects of the education process. Curriculum design is a key function in this process. Teachers who are critical and apply a transformation approach as prescribed by Banks (1993) will be able to develop a curriculum of social action and advocacy that celebrates diversity. The purpose of curriculum planning is to plan not only the content for diversity but also the conceptual framework.

Banks' concepts of prejudice reduction and resistance to multicultural curriculum transformation have long been assumed to be a function of faculty racism, sexism, and classicism. Omiunota Ukpokodu (Multicultural Perspectives, 2003), a scholar and active member of NAME, provides both a personal and professional account of the challenges of teaching multicultural education from a critical perspective. Her work, "Teaching Multicultural Education From a Critical Perspective: Challenges and Dilemma," reminds us that our work , when done right, requires that we take professional risks but remain fully grounded in principles of social justice. Multicultural curriculum transformation is an outgrowth of the field of multicultural education, which emerged in the 1970s (Nieto, 2000). During the 1980s and early 1990s, multicultural curriculum transformation rose to the center of the multicultural debates across the country on college campuses (Graff, 1992).

Banks developed books, articles, monographs, guidelines, and materials and resources such as "Teaching Strategies for Ethnic Studies" (1975, 1995), as well as methods and approaches for curriculum inclusion and curriculum reform. He developed strategies for teaching Black Studies before he refocused on multi-ethnic, multi-racial, and multicultural education in the 1970s. The transition occurred as early as 1965 when he wrote about the "Negro Self-Concept and Implications for Education and the Social Sciences."

Banks and Multicultural Curriculum Reform

Leaders in the field of multicultural education generally agree that little significant progress has been made in developing teaching practices and curriculum that meet the needs of culturally, racially, and socially diverse classrooms (Grant & Sleeter, 1988). School districts with little cultural and racial diversity within their student body and teaching staff are usually ill equipped to achieve the goals of multicultural education. The assumption that multicultural education is only important if the school district's population is itself diverse represents a misunderstanding of the importance of providing all students, especially those who have been raised with a strong Anglo-centric cultural and social values, with the understandings and competencies necessary to contribute to achieving the goal of a democratic multicultural society.

Pre-service education is important in bringing this awareness to light and to providing strategies and solutions to developing a multicultural curriculum. Banks defines the goal of multicultural education as that of helping students "develop cross- cultural competency within the American national culture with their own subculture and within and across different sub-societies and cultures" (Banks, 1994, p.

9). The development of such competency involves knowledge of cultural and racial differences and issues; the critical examination of one's beliefs and values regarding culture, race, and social class; and an understanding of how knowledge, beliefs, and values determine one's behavior with respect to minorities.

The primary White and middle-class teachers in our nation's schools are ill prepared in knowledge, skills, and attitude to teach for equity and excellence in multicultural education classrooms. They cannot teach for cross-cultural competency when they lack it themselves. Teacher education programs intent on changing this situation must recognize the necessity of providing learning experiences that increase the likelihood that pre-service teachers will undergo transformative learning regarding multicultural education. Curriculum for pre-service teachers should include an understanding of the relative strengths and weaknesses of the philosophical frameworks and specific multicultural models such as the contributions, additive, transformative and social action.

The Influence of Banks' Theories on Other Multicultural Educators and Curricula

All children differ from one another in their physical attributes and in their ability to learn. Some are taller, some are stronger, some can run fast, and some cannot run at all. Some children learn quickly and can use what they have learned in new situations. The term exceptional students (or exceptional children) includes both children who have difficulty learning and children whose performances is so advanced that an individualized educational program is necessary to meet their needs. The terms disability and handicap have different meanings. The term disability refers to the loss or reduced function of a certain body part or organ. An impairment is often synonymous with disability. A child with a disability cannot perform certain tasks such as walking, speaking, and seeing. A disability is not considered a handicap unless the disability results in educational personal, social, or other problems.

The multicultural education literature and the disability literature each address how to make schools and classrooms more responsive to and supportive of diverse groups of children with special needs (Banks & Banks, 1997). Multicultural education gives the most attention to ethnicity and race, and connections with disability have grown largely out of the problem of overrepresentation of students of color in special education. Having teachers or professors of color who can serve as role models and who understand how to teach culturally diverse students is rewarding to students. The scarcity of educators of color heightens the need for cultural sensitivity by school personnel and aggravates the lack of teachers of color as role models for minorities and students in special education (Gay, 1995c). African American students continue to be over- represented in special education classes and underrepresented in the talented and gifted classes in public schools. Without adequate training, special education teachers are not able to maintain complementary learning environments to meet the needs of students of color in particular (Gay, 1995c). As schools become more culturally diverse, and as collaboration across disciplines and roles becomes more necessary, teachers need more cultural sensitivity in order to assess and work fairly with children.

In 1963, a conference was held at the Lincoln Filene Center at Tufts University in Massachusetts to explore the various dimensions of Black self-identity in children, and increase their academic achievement and emotional growth. The very act of calling together the conference indicated that educators such as Banks were not only becoming increasingly sensitive to the unique problems in Black children's experiences in schools and society, but were searching for creative ways to solve the issues of increasing learning among Black children and People of Color as well. Many Blacks at that time did not prefer the term Negro and opted for the term Black. The issue of racial and ethnic identity is still being debated in the U.S. Bureau of the Census as bi-racial and multi- racial citizens reject the terms of identification currently used in the census. Other categories have recently been added to capture the true cultural identity of Puerto Ricans, African Americans, and those of Caribbean descent, as well as bi-racial, and multi-racial individuals.

Despite the bitter and divisive debates among those for and against multicultural education, major theoretical and conceptual work has been done within the last 20 years (Banks, 1973, 1988a; Sleeter & Grant, 1988). There are many different strategies, definitions, and approaches to multicultural education (Banks & Banks, 1993). At least three major approaches can be identified: curriculum reform, achievement, and inter- group education. Curriculum reform approaches conceptualize multicultural education as a process that involves additions to or changes in the content of the school or university curriculum. The primary goal of these approaches is to incorporate the voices, experiences, and struggles of ethnic, cultural, and gender groups into the curriculum. The various approaches within this category vary greatly in conceptions, goals, and outcomes. Banks proposes the (1) contributions, (2) additive, (3) transformative, and (4) decision making and social action approaches (Banks, 1988b), while other theorists support the achievement approaches as a set of goals, theories, and strategies designed to increase the academic achievement of low-income students of color, women, and students with disabilities.

Critics of Multiculturalism

Some critics of multiculturalism believe that the concept devalues Western civilization or seeks its elimination from the curriculum (e.g., Ravitch, 1990). There is no evidence to support this contention, however. Pedagogical components of multicultural teaching have been woven from many different strands such as ethnic studies, feminist pedagogy, liberatory education, and interactive and experimental learning methods (Sleeter & Grant, 1987).

Ravitch (1990) distinguished between the cultural pluralist and the particularistic approach to multicultural education. The former "accepts diversity as fact, and the latter seeks to attach students to their ancestral homelands as a source of personal identity and authentic culture" (Ravitch 1990, p. A44). The development of positive identification with an ancestral culture does not constitute a negative consequence of a multicultural curriculum. Banks (1988) suggested that persons must develop positive ethnic identification before they can develop a clarified national identification. The goal of education should be to expose students to a wide range of information and allow them to draw their own conclusions.

A number of authors have written about potentially dangerous elements in multicultural education. In his book, *Illiberal Education,* D'Sousa states that "new forms of criticism" generate "an intellectual free fall" that "directly undermines the notion that traditional academic criteria have any validity." D'Sousa ignores the obvious fact that new scholarship and theories have been and continue to be subjected to endless academic review and debate. A potential danger in this artificial dichotomy is that topics that are legitimate, but may not particularly contribute to the unifying theme, are dismissed as destructive multicultural education. Issues such as institutional racism and linguistics or gender discrimination are the type of topics that are legitimate areas of study, but prime candidates for dismissal as destructive multiculturalism.

The public schools are primarily charged with the role of developing students' ability to think critically about how knowledge in the social, behavioral, and natural sciences is constructed and influenced by the scientists' own racial, cultural, and social class backgrounds. They are also charged with developing pedagogical practices that affirm the lived experiences of all children and to create culturally compatible classroom practices (Banks, 1995, p. 45).

Barbara Farmer's Chapter on Diversity Begins at home (Farmer, 2003), "Provides the "real deal" on the importance of the family in framing the differences created with others.

CHAPTER 3

Methodology

The purpose of this study was to introduce, support and validate the need for a multicultural education and diversity course in Colleges of Education based on the framework and the works of James A. Banks, and other multicultural education theorists. The strategic plan in the Penn State College of Education (1998-2003) supports the need for more course diversity surrounding issues of race, sexual orientation issues, gay, lesbian, bi-sexual, trans-gender, religion, ethnicity, and equity issues.

It was necessary to develop a plan for problem identification and a needs assessment to collect data for suggestions about teacher training and improvement and developing curriculum reform strategies from students, teachers, professional educators and scholars.

The problem identification and needs assessment were determined via suggestions for the training of teachers from the Pennsylvania State Wide Spring Multicultural

Conference held at Penn State on Saturday, March 31, 2001 (8am to 4pm) at the Penn State Conference Center. The event was also hosted by the Pennsylvania Chapter of the National Association of Multicultural Education (PA_ NAME), the College of Education at Penn State, the Office of the Vice Provost for Equity Education, and the Office of Undergraduate Education.

The researcher wondered why more courses on race and ethnicity identity were not more available for College of Education students as well as throughout the university. Several such courses are available in the College of the Liberal Arts (Sociology 409 and Inequality in America (Sociology 119) addressing these issues and some additional courses in the Workforce Education Department (Workforce Education 450) have recently emerged. The curriculum and instruction department is responsible for most of the teacher training pre-service courses.

In addition, student reaction to hate crimes, acts of unrest across the country and on college campuses, generated an interest in the ideas about the need for a diversity course for all students in particular students in education. The Pennsylvania Statewide Spring Multicultural Education Conference on Saturday, March 31, 2001, held at Penn State, served as a vehicle for identifying and confirming issues for discussion and development of strategies for curriculum inclusion and reform.

This chapter describes the five stages of the research design, described below:

1. Needs Assessment and Problem Identification;

2. Curriculum Design, Questionnaire and Statewide Conference;

3. Methodology: Population and Participant Analysis for the Diversity Pilot Course;

4. Survey Questionnaire Instrument Analysis and Implementation; and

5. Analysis and Evaluation of the Pilot Course and Questionnaire.

Five Stages of the Research Design Needs Assessment and Problem Identification

As a result of acts of intolerance and incidences of hate mail, racial injustice, and a lack of multicultural curricula in schools across the country, a need was identified for a curriculum and to share educational strategies that would improve upon the lack of understanding and awareness of multicultural education in academic institutions.

Curriculum Design, Questionnaire, and Statewide Conference

Themes for the curriculum design focused on the following types of questions: "What does it mean to be White?" "What does it mean to be American?" "What is multicultural education?" "What's the difference between diversity and multicultural education?" "Should multicultural education or diversity courses be mandatory in curriculum?" "Should all teachers have a course in multicultural education or diversity?" "What are the race, sexual orientation, religious, and diversity issues relevant to teacher education and the community?"

These issues were addressed in the pilot course designed for observation and analysis in this study. "What is White privilege?" These themes were looked at in designing a curriculum to assist higher education pre-service educators in redesigning their teacher education activities to comply with NCATE Standards as suggested by Donna M. Gollnick, G. Pritchy Smith and other educators across the country.

Methodology: Population and Participant Analysis for the Diversity Pilot Course

The curriculum design included a pilot course used to help participants strengthen their knowledge and awareness of reflective practice and activities through video observations, and sharing ideas and strategies for curriculum inclusion using Banks' models for curriculum reform.

Survey Questionnaire Instrument Analysis and Implementation

The pilot questionnaire was administered to students randomly in classes with the assistance and approval of instructors in College of Education CI412 LLED classes. Guest presenters shared strategies for curriculum reform using Banks' models (additive, ethnic contributions, transformative, and social action decision making curriculum inclusion and reform strategies).

Analysis and Evaluation of the Pilot Course and Questionnaire

Participants explored strategies that actively engaged students in multiculturalism through dialogue and reflection. Some of the dialogue sessions were conducted by faculty, staff, and local community members such as: the Jewish Community Center Leader Rabbi, Muslim Association Leader, Eisenhower Chapel Spiritual Leader, Diversity Specialist Consultant College of the Liberal Arts, Multicultural Affairs Director, College of the Liberal Arts, Speech Communications Presenter, College of Arts and

Architecture, Special Assistant to the Vice Provost, Marketing and Diversity Professor, Smeal College of Business, Senior Diversity Specialist, College of Communications, Assistant Dean for Multicultural Affairs, Education Faculty Presenter, Marywood University, President, Interfaith Community Coalition Against Prejudice and Violence and Christian Science Educators, Past President, Women's Commission, Friends of India Member, Adult Education Counselor, Past President, Women's Commission, Senior Diversity Specialist, Student Services and Crime, Law, and Justice Instructor, Student Panel on Hate Crimes and a Community Panel by the Interfaith Community Coalition Against Prejudice and Violence. Some of the objectives of this analysis were to encourage social action and decision making in the students' everyday lives. Another goal was to create activities that are responsive to the needs of students and communities through dialogue, reflection, and feedback. The pilot course questionnaire generated questions that were to be reflected on by the participants and guest presenters.

The expected outcomes from the study included the notion that students, staff, faculty, community, and administrators, presented with multicultural education concepts and strategies, will be more successful and knowledgeable in implementing collaborative social programs, teacher education programs, pre-service programs, professional development programs, and in-service curriculum inclusion programs. Although the summer enrollment was not measured quantitatively but qualitatively, this pilot course and study can be repeated in the Fall 2003 semester to gain additional data for creating diversity courses or freshman seminars.

Target Population

The second survey research study included the demographic data missing from the first study in 2001 and repeated in 2003—N=150. The survey instrument is displayed in the appendix.

Student participants included Curriculum Instruction students in Language and Literacy (LLED 411 and 412) students, Early Childhood Education (ECE) 451 and 452 participants, Psychology 002 participants, and Field Experience participants in CI495. The students and participants in the pilot course included regular Penn State matriculating registrants and State College volunteer community participants. The matriculating participants included undergraduates and community members and many others who participated throughout the course.

Procedure

Each class presentation was videotaped for feedback and documentation, each participant gave written reflections on the course during in-class interviews and each guest presenter provided oral and written feedback on how their presentation was integrated into the four curriculum reform models (ethnic contributions, additive, transformative, and decision making social action). The instructor/researcher also invited outside observers from the College of Education to provide feedback and insight. Each guest presenter was given a letter of appreciation from the Dean of the College of Education and the President of Penn State for their participation in the diversity pilot summer course.

Focus Groups

Four focus groups from the Pennsylvania NAME (National Association of Multicultural Education) Statewide Pre-Conference (March 31, 2001) were used to generate the desired information for the pilot course and survey research design.

The assignments were given to the four randomly selected focus groups charged to develop strategies and discuss solutions for achieving curriculum integration and multicultural education in schools and colleges, and to review and discuss ways to accomplish diversity at other institutions regarding and including issues on race, ethnicity, religion, sexual orientation, diversity at respective institutions. All proceedings are available at C-Net Public Education Television in State College, Pa. The four focus groups were videotaped by C-Net Public Education television, as was the keynote address given by the guest presenter from North Carolina State University, Ashville, North Carolina, and the presentation by Dean of the College of Education Climate Diversity Co-Chair, and conference organizer, proposal developer, writer, and researcher, Andrew Jackson, Sr. Group A was designated by randomly assigned badges with a red dot and was led by a College of Education Faculty member and Continuing and Distance Education Client Management member; Group B was randomly assigned badges with a yellow dot and was led by a College of Agricultural Sciences faculty member and Staff Education Coordinator for Eisenhower Auditorium; Group C was randomly assigned badges with a green dot and was led by the Assistant Dean for the Undergraduate Education Office and International Programs, and Associate Professor of Education from Kutztown University; and Group D was randomly assigned badges with a blue dot and was led by the Director of the Student Support Services Program at Penn State, Director of Urban Education at Millersville University, and NAME National Coordinator. The guest presenter, a faculty member, University of North Carolina, College of Education Climate Diversity Committee Co-Chair and Professor of Work Force Education, Penn State, and the researcher acted as roaming facilitators to keep the groups focused on the task. There were 25 participants in each of the four focus groups with a cross between higher education and public education professionals and students. Over 100 participants registered for the conference hosted by the Penn State Conference Center, who also compiled the evaluation and feedback summary that was used in the final report to the College of Education, Office of Outreach, and Office of Equity Education, and compiled by the Conference and Institutes Office and conference participants.

The multiple focus groups used in the Pennsylvania NAME Spring 2001 Statewide conference at the Penn Stater Conference Center provided the back up information for future follow up, in combination with the videotapes by C-Net. The use of multiple groups was considered by the researcher to generate a broader variety of ideas (Babbie, 1998, p. 2480). The group size was recommended by Stewart and Shadasani (1990, p. 57). The proceedings were shared in the College of Education Climate and Diversity Report for 2002-2003 as a response to the "Plan for Fostering Diversity".

A follow-up conference to develop a broader collection of feedback and outreach on "Building Bridges" on issues or race, ethnicity, discrimination, prejudice, racism, religion, and diversity issues was developed for May 17 and 18, 2002 in Pittsburgh, Pennsylvania at Carlow College. The featured presenters were Valerie Oak Pang, and a panel of educators from the Western Region of NAME.

The next phase of the research design involved the design and implementation of a pilot diversity course evaluation model for analysis and to implement the strategies and suggestions suggested from the focus groups. These activities were developed using James Banks' model for ethnic curriculum contributions, additive curriculum content, transformative action for school reform, and decision making for social action in the curriculum inclusion model. The Office of Compliance and Human Subjects at Penn State approved the survey questionnaire and approved the study study for research in a diversity course, Multicultural Education Perspectives: ED 197A:

A Dialogue in Race, Sexual Orientation, Religion, Ethnicity, and Diversity Issues in Education and the Community (in appendix D: Multicultural Perspectives.

CHAPTER 4

Findings

The data used in formulating findings in this chapter were taken from the 15-item survey research instrument administered by this researcher, and described in chapter 3. (The survey instrument can be found in the Appendix A: Survey Research Instrument). The sample population was composed of 150 individuals at The Pennsylvania State University (Penn State) who completed the survey with the approval of the instructors in Psychology 002 classes, Language and Literacy classes (LLED 411 and 412), Early Childhood Education classes (ECE 451 and 452), and Clinical Supervised Field Experience classes (CI 495 Field Experience). The re-test was administered after two weeks to students in Psychology 002, sections 1 and 2, in the Continuing Education evening class. A total of 112 female participants (74.7%) and 38 male participants (25.3%) were included in the survey research. A statement-by-statement analysis was conducted of survey items 1–15.

Findings described in this chapter are related to each of the four research questions. The analysis and data are depicted via tables to provide insight into the demographic characteristics of the respondents. This chapter discusses the research findings from the data analysis with an additional goal of sharing a strategy for creating and designing a multicultural education curriculum intervention and implementation in a new diversity course.

The survey research data collection and model for adding a diversity component in pre-service teacher training in the College of Education at Penn State was one of the intended outcomes. The researcher sought to prove a hypothesis (H1), that "students receiving more information on diversity and multicultural education issues in pre-service teacher training will be more knowledgeable about multicultural education in schools and the workplace environment than students who have not received any additional course work or training in multicultural education and diversity."

The strategies utilized in the study were modified from the curriculum reform and inclusion models developed by James A. Banks.

The four questions that guided this study were modified from the original study questions in order to elicit and interpret the responses reflected in the data analysis. The research questions and findings appropriate to each are reported below.

Research Question 1

What are the relative strengths and weaknesses of Banks' teacher education training compared to those of other prominent multicultural education theorists? Did race, sex, ethnicity, or gender affect the students' responses?

As shown in the literature review (chapter 2), Banks' teacher education training theories are consistent with those of other educators and theorists such as Christine Sleeter, Carl Grant, Sonia Nieto, and others who believe that Race, Sex, Gender, and Ethnicity should be discussed as part of the teacher education curriculum. Tables 1-6 highlight responses from students to Survey Items 1, 2, 3, 4, 5, and 6, respectively.

Table 1.
Students indicated their understanding of multicultural education
(*N*=150)

Response	Strongly Disagree 1	Disagree 2	Undecided 3	Agree 4	Strongly Agree 5
Percentage	2.0 (3 of 150)	23.3 (35 of 150)	33.3 (50 of 150)	37.3 (56 of 150)	4.0 (6 of 150)

Total: 100%

Note: 41.3% of the respondents agreed with question 1.

Table 2.

Students who had taken more than one diversity or multicultural course
(*N*=150)

Response	Strongly Disagree 1	Disagree 2	Undecided 3	Agree 4	Strongly Agree 5
Percentage	30.7 46 of 150) (Adjusted)	24.7 (37 of 150)	12.7 (19 of 150)	12.0 18 of 150)	18.7 (28 of 150)s

Total: 100%

Note: Data in Table 2 indicated that 30.7 % of the respondents agree with question 2.

Table 3.

Students indicated that race influences teaching style
(*N*=150)

Response	Strongly Disagree 1	Disagree 2	Undecided 3	Agree 4	Strongly Agree 5
Percentage	14.7 (22 of 150)	22.7 (34 of 150)	27.3 (41 of 150)	28.7 43 of 150)	6.0 9 of 150)

Total: 100%

Note: Responses to Statement 3 indicate that 34.7% agree with question 3.

Table 4.

Students indicated that gender influences teaching style (N=150)

Response	Strongly Disagree 1	Disagree 2	Undecided 3	Agree 4	Strongly Agree 5
Percentage	14.0 (21 of 150)	34.0 (36 of 150)	20.7 (31 of 150)	34.0 (51 of 150)	6.7 (10 of 150)

Total: 100%

Note: 40.7% of the respondents agreed with this question.

Table 5.

Students indicated that ethnicity influences teaching style (N=150)

Response	Strongly Disagree 1	Disagree 2	Undecided 3	Agree 4	Strongly Agree 5
Percentage	11.3 (17 of 150)	20 (30 of 150)	24 (36 of 150)	39.3 (59 of 150)	4.0 (6s of 150)

Total: 100%

Note: 43.3 % of the respondents agreed with question 5.

Table 6.

Students indicated that social class influences teaching style (*N*=150)

Response	Strongly Disagree 1	Disagree 2	Undecided 3	Agree 4	Strongly Agree 5
Percentage	13.3 (20 of 150)	18.0 (27 of 150)	30.7 (46 of 150)	30.0 (45 of 150)	8.0 (12 of 150)

Total: 100%

Note: 38 % of the respondents agreed with question 6.

Summary of Survey Items 1-6

The findings from Survey Items 1, 2, 3, 4, 5, and 6 revealed the following:

1. Less than 50% (41.3%) of the respondents agreed to have had an understanding of multicultural education. This small percentage could support the need for more courses or instruction in understanding multicultural education in the curriculum.

2. Less than 50% of the respondents (30.9%) agreed to take more than one diversity course. In order for student demographics to reflect global awareness in society, additional diversity and multicultural education courses should be included in the curriculum or

opportunities should be made available to increase the awareness of diversity in the curriculum.

3. Only 34% of the respondents felt that race influences their teaching style. While race should not influence teaching style, students should be aware of the difference between race and ethnicity as it relates to identity and understanding of different culture groups.

4. Less than 50% of the respondents (40.7%) agreed that gender influences teaching style. Gender should not influence teaching style overall, but teachers and students should be aware of different gender influences on individuals as well as gay, lesbian, transgender, and ethnicity issues that could affect student interaction and understanding in the classroom between the sexes.

5. 43% of the respondents agreed that ethnicity influences teaching style. Ethnicity should not influence teaching styles overall, although students and teachers should be aware of the different ethnicities in the class and their implications for cross-cultural similarities and differences with respect to holiday observances, individual and group sensitivity, and cross-cultural inter-group and intra-group communications in the classroom.

6. Only 38% of the respondents agreed that socioeconomic status influences teaching style. Socioeconomic status of the teacher or students should not affect teaching styles, although educators should be aware of inequalities in communities with respect to access to computer equipment, transportation, food, clothing and shelter among low income students and the effects and influences of inequality on learning and the development of cross-cultural competency in schools and the workplace.

Research Question 2

Can a multicultural education course using Banks' work be designed and delivered during a fall, spring, or summer session course, through which students transition through Banks' four stages of curriculum reform and curriculum intervention understanding? Would students be willing to take another multicultural education or diversity course not required?

Survey Items 7, 8, 9, and 10 reflect supportive responses to the above research question. Findings are revealed in Tables 7–10, respectively.

Table 7.

Do you feel that faculty have a sincere interest in the inclusion of multicultural education and diversity in the curriculum?

(N=150)

Response	Strongly Disagree 1	Disagree 2	Undecided 3	Agree 4	Strongly Agree 5
Percentage	6.0 (1 of 150)	16.0 (24 of 150)	32.7 (49 of 150)	36.0 (54 of 150)	8.0 (12 of 150)

Total: 100%

Note: 44% of the respondents agreed with this statement.

Table 8.

Do you feel that diversity courses enhance your knowledge and understanding of multicultural education?

(N=150)

Response	Strongly Disagree 1	Disagree 2	Undecided 3	Agree 4	Strongly Agree 5
Percentage	1.3 (2 of 150)	2.0 (3 of 150)	6.7 (10 of 150)	45.3 (60 of 150)	43.3 (65 of 150)

Total: 100%

Note: 88.6% of the respondents agreed with this question.

Table 9.

Do you feel you have had at least one course on multicultural education available as part of your curriculum?

(N=150)

Response	Strongly Disagree 1	Disagree 2	Undecided 3	Agree 4	Strongly Agree 5
Percentage	14.0 (21 of 150)	12.0 (18 of 150)	18.7 (28 of 150)	23.3 (35 of 150)	31.3 (47 of 150)

Total: 100%

Note: *54.6 % of the respondents agreed with question 9.*

Table 10.

Would you be willing to take an additional course to discuss and learn about multicultural education issues?
(*N*=150)

Response	Strongly Disagree 1	Disagree 2	Undecided 3	Agree 4	Strongly Agree 5
Percentage	6.0 (9 of 150)	4.7 (7 of 150)	22.0 (33 of 150)	38.7 (58 of 150)	28.0 (42 of 150)

Total: 100%

Note: *66.7% of the respondents agreed with question #10.*

Summary of Survey Items 7-10

Findings for survey items 7, 8, 9, and 10 revealed the following:

1. For survey item 7, only 44% of the respondents (fewer than 50%) agreed that faculty members have a sincere interest in the inclusion of multicultural edu-

cation and diversity in the curriculum. This should not mean that more than 50% of the respondents feel that faculty do not have a sincere interest in diversity and multicultural education but that faculty need to do a better job of sharing that interest through guest lectures and seminars that reflect their interests and should make available courses with curriculum content that reflects diversity and knowledge of multicultural issues.

2. For item 8, 88.6% of the respondents agreed that diversity courses enhance their cross-cultural knowledge and awareness of multicultural education. Diversity and multicultural education can be delivered by films such as "the Color of Fear by Mun Whah" (Stir Fry Productions) and follow-up workshops, interdisciplinary and multidisciplinary curriculum strategies, music, arts, and writing.

3. For item 9, 54.6% of the respondents agreed that they have had at least one course on multicultural education. It is up to programs and administrators to get together with faculty to decide on a process for incorporating diversity and multicultural education into the curriculum as a valued component of the students' education.

4. For item 10, although 67% of the respondents felt

that they would be willing to take an additional course to learn about multicultural education and diversity issues as a start, learning about diversity is a process that involves more than one course. It takes more than one course to learn about the historical roots of diversity and multicultural education but taking one course is a start. It is important to offer more diversity awareness training or education for those students who may not have had any awareness of diversity issues prior to higher education. Diversity awareness should start from students' elementary, junior high or middle school education prior to their higher education experiences.

Research Question 3

What are the implications of Bank' models for multicultural education in the design of a multicultural course for teachers in a College of Education? Do students feel ethnicity affects their teaching styles?

Survey items 11, 12, 13, 14, and 15 were designed to elicit students' perceptions of White students and Students of Color in teaching each other. Findings are shown in Tables 11–15, respectively.

According to the data contained in Table 11, about half the respondents felt that adequate books, films, articles, and educational resources are available to them in the library on

multicultural education, although 42.5% remained undecided, while only 11% disagreed.

Table 11.

Do you feel there are adequate books, articles, magazines,
films, and educational resources available to you on multicultural education?
(N=150)

Response	Strongly Disagree 1	Disagree 2	Undecided 3	Agree 4	Strongly Agree 5
Percentage	4.0 (6 of 150)	24.7 (37 of 150)	32.7 (49 of 150)	30.7 (46 of 150)	6.7 (10 of 150)

Total: 100%
*Note: 52% of the respondents agreed that there are adequate
books, films, articles, and educational sources available to them.*

Table 12.
Do you feel that students are being prepared to face the cross-
cultural challenges of the New Millennium?
(N=150)

Response	Strongly Disagree 1	Disagree 2	Undecided 3	Agree 4	Strongly Agree 5
Percentage	7.0 (1 of 150)	4.0 (6 of 150)	42.7 (64 of 150)	32.0 (48 of 150)	20.0 (30 of 150)

Total: 100%

Note: 37.4 % of the respondents agreed that students are being prepared to face the cross-cultural challenges of the New Millennium. Two item responses are missing.

Table 13.

Do you feel that White students are uncomfortable teaching ethnic minorities and People of Color?

(N=150)

Response	Strongly Disagree 1	Disagree 2	Undecided 3	Agree 4	Strongly Agree 5
Percentage	15.3 (23 of 150)	40.0 (60 of 150)	31.3 (47 of 150)	7.3 (11 of 150)	2.7 4 of 150)

Total: 100%

Note: 28% of the respondents feel that White students are uncomfortable teaching ethnic minorities and People of Color. Two responses are missing.

Table 14.

Do you feel that Students of Color are uncomfortable teaching White students?

(N=150)

Response	Strongly Disagree 1	Disagree 2	Undecided 3	Agree 4	Strongly Agree 5
Percentage	12.0 (18 of 150)	33.3 (50 of 150)	35.3 (53 of 150)	14.0 (21 of 150)	4.0 (6 of 150)

Total: 100%

Note: Only 10% of the respondents feel that Students of Color are uncomfortable teaching White students. Five responses are missing.

Table 15.

Do you feel that all students have an opportunity for cross-cultural interaction in their classes?

N=150

Response	Strongly Disagree 1	Disagree 2	Undecided 3	Agree 4	Strongly Agree 5
Percentage	4.0 (6 of 150)	16.0 (24 of 150)	20.0 (30 of 150)	43.3 (65 of 150)	14.0 214 of 150)

Note: 57.3 % of the respondents feel that students have an opportunity for cross-cultural interaction in their classes. Nine responses are missing.

Summary of Survey Items 11-15

The findings from survey items 11, 12, 13, 14, and 15 revealed the following:

1. For survey item 11, although 52% of the respondents agreed, 11% disagreed and 42.7% remained undecided about the adequacy of books, articles, etc. The majority believed, however, that there are adequate books, articles, magazines, films, and edu-

cational resources available to them on multicultural education.

2. For survey item 12, the indicators are that less than 50% of the respondents believed that students feel they are being prepared to face the cross-cultural challenges of the New Millennium and the 21st Century. A total of 37.4% agreed, 32.7% remained undecided, and only 28.7% disagreed. Perhaps faculty and staff can do a better job of making students feel more positive by generating a more welcoming climate and making available more courses, cross-cultural activities, workshops, and seminars on multicultural education and diversity.

3. For survey item 13, it may be that some students were uncomfortable with this question or did not feel safe revealing their true feelings—it is difficult to gauge this without asking about these feelings directly. A qualitative follow up could ask students how they felt about answering this question. This survey found that less than 50% of the respondents disagreed, 35.3% were undecided, and only 18% agreed that White students are uncomfortable teaching ethnic minorities or Students of Color.

4. For survey item 14, the researcher reversed question 13 to see if some consistency existed that also indi-

cated that Students of Color are not uncomfortable teaching White students. A high number of students disagreed (55.3%). A total of 31.3% were undecided and only 10% agreed.

5. For survey item 15, this question indicated that only 20% disagreed or believed that all students had an opportunity for cross-cultural interaction in their classes. A total of 20% were undecided while 57% agreed with this question.

Research Question 4

To what extent does Banks' approach to multicultural education provide concrete guidelines for teacher training? Do students feel their diversity and multicultural education training will prepare them for the 21ˢᵗ Century and the New Millennium?

Banks believes that students should learn about curriculum integration and inclusion based on his additive model of curriculum reform, ethnic contributions model of curriculum reform, transformative model of curriculum reform, and decision making social action model of curriculum reform. Survey results provide an overview of the respondents' thinking about diversity and multicultural education issues. These findings may be considered in developing a curriculum that addresses issues of race, gender, and ethnicity.

The primary goal of a course in multicultural education and diversity is to assist people in competently interacting, teaching, and working with those who are different on several levels, including cross-culturally, racially, ethnically, gender, religion, and class, and yet share inherent human similarities. Most multicultural education programs or courses are based on the core belief that prejudices, discrimination, and inter-group/intercultural conflict are primarily a result of ignorance, lack of awareness, lack of accurate information about people, misinformation, or misperceptions.

Summary

The researcher believes that this study parallels the diversity efforts of Penn State and the College of Education in carrying out their strategic plan for 2004 and beyond by making suggestions for strategies to enhance the development of more knowledge in multicultural education and diversity by an additional course, workshop, or training for educators.

Penn State, like other American colleges and universities, is charged with creating an environment characterized by equal access for all students, faculty, and staff regardless of cultural differences, where individuals are not just tolerated but valued.

Penn State's mission statement parallels that of other campus missions in suggesting that higher education institutions value multicultural awareness and understanding within an environment of mutual respect and cooperation. Penn

State's strategic planning framework (College of Education Diversity Climate Committee Report, 2003) articulates the goal of the University to become "a caring University community that provides leadership for constructive participation in a diverse multicultural world" (College of Education, Diversity Strategic Plan, 2003, p. 1).

Several sampled students provided qualitative data that indicates their reflections about the summer pilot diversity course at Penn State. The qualitative responses mirror the quantitative responses in survey item 1, which indicated that students have an adequate understanding of multicultural education, and survey item 2, which indicated that students have had at least one diversity course. Survey item 3 indicated that students did not feel that race influences their teaching style. Survey item 4 indicated that gender does not and should not influence teaching style. Survey item 5 indicated that ethnicity does not and should not influence teaching style, according to this researcher.

Survey item 6 indicates that respondents believe that social economic status did not influence teaching style according to the respondents. However, this researcher believes that access to educational experiences is affected by social economic status and resources available for travel, computer equipment, and other educational opportunities. Survey item 7 positively indicated that students do believe that faculty members have a sincere interest in the inclusion of multicultural education and diversity in the curriculum. This researcher believes that this area can be enhanced by the availability of courses, workshops, and other interdisciplinary strategies for teaching multicultural education such as the arts, music, theater, films, and counseling encounter groups. Survey item 8 indicates that the respondents believe that diversity courses enhance their knowledge and understanding of multicultural education. Survey item 9 indicates that students have had at least one multicultural education or diversity course. Additional research might suggest that there are different interpretations of multicultural education or diversity courses, such as race and ethnicity, religion, cross cultural awareness, gender issues, and other areas of diversity. This concept should be clearly defined for all educators and students to parallel understanding and interpretations. Survey item 10 indicates that students would be willing to take an additional diversity course to learn about multicultural education.

Survey item 11 indicates that students or respondents believe there are adequate books, films, articles, and educational resources available to them in the library on multicultural education to learn about multicultural education and diversity. Survey item 12 indicated that students believe they are being prepared to face the cross-cultural challenges of the New Millennium and the 21st Century. Survey item 13 indicated that White students believe they are comfortable teaching ethnic minorities and students of color. Survey item 14 indicated that respondents believe that students of color are comfortable teaching White students. Survey item 15 indicated that students believe they have an opportunity for cross-cultural interaction in their classes.

Reflections from students regarding their participation and additional comments are noted in Appendix B: Pilot Course Student Reflections.

CHAPTER 5

Summary, Conclusions, and Recommendations

This study examined specific teacher education recommendations for curriculum development with the central focus on multicultural education as viewed in the works of James A. Banks, Professor of Multicultural Education (MCE) for the training of teachers at the University of Washington, Seattle, Washington. This study also provided information on the perspectives of multicultural educators and focused on specific teacher education recommendations for developing curriculum.

Purpose

The purpose of this study was to introduce, support and validate the need for a multicultural education and diversity course in the College of Education based on the framework and the works of James A. Banks, and other multicultural education theorists. The strategic plan in the Penn State College of Education (1998–2003) supports the need for more course diversity surrounding issues of race, sexual orientation issues, gay, lesbian, bi-sexual, trans-gender, religion, ethnicity, and equity issues.

The data validated the need to establish more multicultural education and diversity in the teacher education programs and to share the results of the survey instrument and pilot course which responded to the four research questions on the need for multicultural education, curriculum reform, and diversity in the curriculum content knowledge base. This researcher believes that a variety of innovative approaches and strategies in multicultural education are being developed and require more systematic training for the new millennium.

The study examined the multicultural perceptions of undergraduate students in the College of Education at Penn State, University Park. Educators can use the results of this study to develop multicultural education programs and activities that correlate with those currently being proposed and implemented in the College of Education and Penn State community. The results of the study can help new and experienced teachers and instructors, administrators, staff, and faculty, in evaluating, measuring, and monitoring their current diversity practices when compared with the backdrop of this study. A summary of the procedures utilized in the study with conclusions, and recommendations are presented in this chapter.

Summary of Procedures

The data for this study were collected through a research survey administered to 150 participants (112 females and 38 males) with follow-up data analysis and evaluation of survey results. The survey contained 15 survey items regarding multicultural education and diversity issues. The survey items were all based on a 5-point Likert Scale from 1–5 with 1 being the lowest rating and 5 being the highest (1-strongly disagree, 2- disagree, 3-undecided, 4-agree, 5-strongly agree). There was also a summary of the modified survey items taken from the four original research questions to elicit the additional data and demographic data required in the study with a summary of findings concerned with addressing these questions.

Research Questions

1. What are the implications of Banks' model for multicultural education in the design of a multicultural course for teachers in a College of Education?

2. What are the relative strengths and weaknesses of

Banks' Teacher Training Recommendations compared to those of other prominent multicultural theorists?

3. Can a multicultural education course using Banks' theories and research be designed and delivered during a summer, fall, or spring session, in which students transition through Banks' stages of multicultural awareness and curriculum reform understanding?

4. To what extent does Banks' approaches to curriculum reform inclusion and multicultural education aware-ness provide concrete guidelines for teacher training?

There were 150 respondents who completed the survey from selected classes at Penn State in the College of Education with the permission of the instructors in Psychology 002, Curriculum and Instruction 495 Field Experiences, Early Childhood Education 451 and 452, and Language and Literacy Education 411 and 412.

In addition to the research survey study, a pilot course was administered in May 2001–June 22, 2001 in 112 Keller Building from 3:55pm to 5:10pm to field test James A. Banks' teaching strategies and concepts on curriculum reform and inclusion. Guest lecturers added to the diversity of the presentations in the pilot multicultural education course by sharing their expert experience on multicultural education and diversity issues.

Conclusions

The findings in this study indicated the following: the respondents did not feel overwhelmingly that race, socio-economic status, ethnicity, or gender influence teaching style; students would be willing to take an additional multicultural education or diversity course to learn about cross-cultural differences; students have had at least one course in diversity or multicultural education; and students feel that a course in diversity or multicultural education would enhance their knowledge and awareness of diversity and multicultural education. The respondents in the study also indicated that White students feel comfortable teaching Students of Color and that Students of Color feel comfortable teaching White students.

The survey responses parallel the feedback from students in the diversity and multicultural education pilot class, June 14, 2001–May 22, 2001.

Recommendations

1. Students should take a required course in the College of Education on race and ethnicity issues in education to enhance their cross-cultural knowledge base. *Rationale*: Faculty, staff, administrators, students, and community members need to keep abreast of recent trends concerning race, ethnicity, sex, gender, issues

that affect our understanding and awareness of issues in education and the community.

2. Students should demonstrate and document knowledge of other races and cultures in a class, workshop, interdisciplinary training, or seminar taught by College of Education faculty. Rationale: As Gary Howard said in his book, *We Can't Teach What We Don't Know*, and Lisa Delpit indicated in her book, *Other People's Children*, it is becoming increasing necessary to have an awareness and understanding of other people's children in our society and to be aware of the issues that affect all children in schools and colleges.

3. Students should document and validate any international or cross-cultural experiences or be encouraged to obtain such experiences. *Rationale*: It is becoming increasingly necessary for students to relate to each other cross-culturally in schools as well as adults in the workplaces across the country. Students should demonstrate practical field experiences working with cross-cultural populations, students, or community members.

4. Students, faculty, staff, and administrators should document an annual workshop, course, or seminar on understanding others issues to prevent negative con-

frontations surrounding race, sex, and gender issues. *Rationale*: We need to show validation of our efforts to show professional growth as well as an awareness of our understanding of all people as a way of valuing diversity in schools and the workplace from a supportive knowledge base.

5. Faculty, administrators, students and staff should be encouraged to provide a welcoming environment in all classrooms, offices, and community areas by showing respect, politeness, and professionalism at all times. *Rationale*: This thinking is based on documented incidents in the Diversity Climate College of Education findings (*Framework to Foster Diversity Final Report*, College of Education, 1999–2003).

6. The university and college need to define their position on the requirement for students to take a uniform course dealing with race, sex, gender, and ethnicity as a diversity or intercultural course requirement. *Rationale*: Without significant intercultural contact, people's perceptions of individuals representing other racial/ethnic groups are more often than not based on faulty information (Ponterotto & Pedersen, 1993, p. 28). As a result, multicultural education efforts have focused primarily on creating accurate information about other cultures in schools and the workplace.

At universities, multicultural education efforts have largely been molded to fit into already existing standard education formats. This has resulted in criticism that most multicultural training programs overemphasize cognitive approaches, rely heavily on traditional intellectual teaching approaches such as formal lectures, and assignments and underemphasize experiential training and life experiences (Ramsey, 1999).

In a recent *Daily Collegian* article (December 10, 2003), Penn State President Graham Spanier stated that, "the recent bias underscores the continuing need to educate students about multiculturalism . . . The recent incident involving the Republican student organization leaders' offensive Web site pictures, was very disturbing to me and everyone else in the administration." He was referring to controversial pictures posted on the Web site of the College Republican chair, which raised concerns regarding the effectiveness of the General Education Intercultural requirement.

In response to several hate and bias incidents that have occurred across the country (e.g., Auburn University, University of Virginia, University of Tennessee at Knoxville, Union College, University of Wisconsin at Whitewater, University of Oklahoma, University of Mississippi, Penn State), there is a need for more multicultural education training and awareness in schools and work environments. Having these courses available and engaging in them may help diffuse some misunderstandings and lack of cross-cultural awareness in schools, colleges, universities, and workplaces. (*www.tolerance.org/images* action/answer.jsp?p=o&id=26).

Recommendations for Further Study

Consideration should be given to replicate this study with administrators, staff, and faculty, as well as graduate, international, and undergraduate students, to determine a broader sampling of students throughout the Commonwealth, in public schools, colleges, and universities. This study consisted of a target group of mostly all Penn State undergraduate students with a few graduate and international student respondents. *Rationale*: As curriculum changes and offerings of diversity global and intercultural courses are taking place in education as well as in the private sectors to reflect feedback, concerns, consideration and input from our racially, ethnically, culturally, socially, and politically diverse populations thinking, there is a greater need for collaboration among educators, administrators, students, and community members involving education strategies for developing a more supportive community among all groups. Employability skills and standards continue to change due to our international and global awareness; therefore, new and up-to-date teaching strategies and new training programs are needed to address common issues among all groups. Services and activities in the past that supported learners as a way to retain students in colleges, schools and the workforce, need to be reviewed and up graded. All these services and programs in schools and the workplace need additional resources and funding to carry out the goals set forth by the administration, students, staff and faculty. Competition is becoming fiercer for scarce resources and funding is divided among more groups and individuals. Creative ways for an equitable distribution of technology, computer equipment and academic resources need to be developed to enhance equity among all groups. No student or worker should be left behind!

References

Akbar, N. (1976). *The community of self* Jersey City, NJ: New Mind Productions.

Akbar, N. (1977). *Natural psychology and human transformation.* Jersey City, NJ: New Mind Productions.

Akbar, N. (1982). *From mis-education to education.* Jersey City, NJ: New Mind Productions.

Allen, T.W. (1994). *The invention of the White race: Racial oppression and social control* (Vol. 1). New York: Verso.

Allport, G. W. (1954). *The nature of prejudice.* Garden City, NY: Doubleday Anchor.

Allport, G.W. (1979). (2nd ed.). *The nature of prejudice.* Reading, MA: Addison-Wesley.

American Council on Education. (1995). *Thirteenth annual status report on minorities in higher education.* Washington, DC: ACE.

Ancheta, A. N. (1998). *Race, rights and Asian American experience.* Piscataway, NJ: Rutgers University Press.

Andersen, J. D. (1988). *The education of blacks in the south, 1860–1935*. Chapel Hill, NC: The University of North Carolina Press.

Andersen, M. L., & Collins, P. H. (1992). *Race, class, and gender: An anthology.* Belmont, CA: Wadsworth.

Andrews, G. R. (1980). *The Afro-Argentines of Buenos Aires, 1800–1900.* Madison, WI: University of Wisconsin Press.

Anzaldua, G. (1987). *Borderlands/La Frontera: The new Mestiza.* San Francisco, CA: Ante Lute Press.

Apple, M.W. (1993). *Official knowledge: Democratic education in a conservative age.* New York: Routledge.

Appleton, N. (1983). *Cultural pluralism in education: Theoretical foundations.* New York: Longman.

Arboleda, T. (1998). *In the shadow of race: Growing up as a multiethnic, multicultural, and multiracial American.* Mahwah, NJ: Lawrence Erlbaum Associates.

Asante, M. K., & Mattson, M. T. (1992). *Historical and cultural atlas of African Americans.* New York: Macmillan Publishing Co.

Asante, M. K. (1987). *The Afrocentric idea.* Philadelphia: Temple University Press.

Asante, M. K. (1990). *Kemet, Afrocentricity and knowledge.* Trenton, NJ. Africa World Press.

Asante, M. K. (1991, Spring). The Afrocentric idea in education. In D. Bragaw & W.S. Thomson (Eds.), *Multicultural education: A global approach* (pp. 261–267). New York: American Forum for Global Education.

Au, K.H. (1993). *Literacy instruction in multicultural settings.* New York: Harcourt Brace College Publishers (Holt, Rinehart, and Winston).

Austin, A. D. (1984). *African Muslims in antebellum America: A sourcebook*. New York: Garland Press.

Baker, G.C. (1977). *Multicultural education: Two In-service approaches. Journal of Teacher Education*, 28, 31–33.

Baker, H. A., Jr. (1993). *Black studies, rap and the academy.* Chicago: University of Chicago Press.

Banks, C. M. (1995). Intellectual leadership and the influence of early African American scholars on multicultural education. *Educational Policy, 9*(3), 260–280.

Banks, J. A. (1967a). Why teachers are dissatisfied. *Phi Delta Kappan*, 48(March), 354.

Banks, J. A. (1967b). Art in social studies. *Illinois Schools Journal, 47*(Fall), 171–174.

Banks, J. A. (1967c). Searching for the unknown. *The Arithmetic Teacher, 14*(December), 683, 689.

Banks, J. A. (1969a) A content analysis of the Black American in textbooks. *Social Education, 33,* 954–957.

Banks, J. A. (1969b). The need for positive racial attitudes in textbooks. In R. L. Green (Ed.), *Racial crisis in American education* (pp. 167–185). Chicago, IL: Follett Press.

Banks, J. A. (1969c). Relevant social studies for Black pupils. *Social Education, 33,* 66– 69.

Banks, J. A. (1969d). A content analysis of elementary history textbooks: The treatment of the Negro and race relations. Ph.D. study, Michigan State University (ProQuest).

Banks, J. A. (1970a). Developing racial tolerance with literature on the black inner city. *Social Education, 34,* 549–552.

Banks, J. A. (1970b). *Teaching the Black experience methods and materials.* Belmont, CA: Fearon.

Banks, J. A. (1971a). The causes of prejudice. In J. A. Banks & W.

W. Joyce (Eds.), *Teaching social studies to culturally different pupils* (pp. 219–225). Reading, MA: Addison-Wesley.

Banks, J. A. (1971b). Social research: Studying racial behavior. In J. A. Banks & W. W. Joyce (Eds.), *Teaching social studies to culturally different pupils* (pp. 219–225). Reading, MA: Addison-Wesley.

Banks, J. A. (1971c). Teaching Black history with a focus on decision making. *Social Education, 35*, 740–745, 820–821.

Banks, J. A. (1971d). Teaching ethnic minority studies with a focus on culture. *Educational Leadership, 29*, 113–117.

Banks, J. A. (1971e). Varieties of history: Negro, black, white. In J. A. Banks & W. W. Joyce (Eds.), *Teaching social studies to culturally different pupils* (pp. 329–332). Reading, MA: Addison-Wesley.

Banks, J. A. (1972a). The destruction of black schools: An American tragedy. *Educational Leadership, 30*, 269–271.

Banks, J. A. (1972b). Imperatives in ethnic minority education. *Phi Delta Kappan, 53*, 266–269.

Banks, J. A. (1972c). Liberating the black ghetto: Decision making and social action. In R. Wisnewski (Ed.), *Teaching about life in the city (42nd Yearbook of the National Council for the Social Studies)* (pp. 150–183). Washington, DC: National Educational Association.

Banks, J. A. (1972d). Racial prejudice and the black self-concept. In J. A. Banks & J. D. Grambs (Eds.), *Black self concept: Implications for education and social science* (pp. 5 – 36). New York: McGraw-Hill.

Banks, J. A. (1972e). Teaching black studies for social change. *Journal of Afro American Issues, 1*, 141 – 164.

Banks, J. A. (1973a). Curriculum strategies for black liberation. *School Review, 81*, 405–414.

Banks, J. A. (1973b). Teaching black studies for social change. In J. A. Banks (Ed.), *Teaching ethnic studies: Concepts and strategies (43rd Yearbook of the National Council for the Social Studies)* (pp. 149–179). Washington, DC: National
Education Association.

Banks, J. A. (Ed.) (1973c). *Teaching ethnic studies: Concepts and strategies (43rd Yearbook of the National Council for the Social Studies)*. Washington, D. C: National Education Association.

Banks, J. A. (1973d). Teaching for ethnic literacy: A comparative approach. *Social Education, 37*, 738–750.

Banks, J. A. (1973e). Teaching strategies for discussion of justice in America: Fact or fiction? *Social Education, 37*, 639–642.

Banks, J. A. (1974a). Cultural pluralism and the schools. *Educational Leadership, 32*, 163–166.

Banks, J. A. (1974b). Increasing teacher competency. In *The final report and recommendations of the Summer Institute on the Improvement and Performance of American Education* (pp. 173–205). Washington, DC: U.S. Department of Health, Education, and Welfare.

Banks, J. A. (1974c). *March toward freedom: A history of Black Americans* (2nd edition) Belmont, CA: Fearon. 2nd ed. First published in 1970.

Banks, J. A. (1975a). Teaching ethnic studies: Key issues and concepts. *Social Studies, 66*, 107–113.

Banks, J. A. (1975b). Should Integration be a societal goal in a pluralistic nation? In R. H. Muessig (Ed.), *Controversial issues in the social studies: A contemporary perspective* (pp. 197–228). Washington, DC: National Council for the Social Studies.

Banks, J. A. (1976a). Crucial issues in the education of Afro American Children. *Journal of Afro American Issues, 4,* 392–407.

Banks, J. A. (1976b). Cultural pluralism and contemporary schools. *Integrated Education, 14*(1), 32–36.

Banks, J. A. (1976c). The emerging stages of ethnicity: Implications for staff development. *Educational Leadership, 34,* 190–193.

Banks, J. A. (1976d). Ethnic studies as a process of curriculum reform. *Social Education, 40,* 76–80.

Banks, J. A. (1976e). Evaluating the multiethnic components of the social studies. *Social Education, 40,* 538–541.

Banks, J. A. (1976f). Pluralism, ideology, and curriculum reform. *Social Studies, 67,* 99–106.

Banks, J. A. (1977a). The implications of multicultural education for teacher education. In F. H. Klassen & D. M. Gollnick (Eds.), *Pluralism and the American teacher: Issues and case studies* (pp. 1–30). Washington, DC: American Association of Colleges for Teacher Education.

Banks, J. A. (1977b). Multiethnic education: Practices and promises. Bloomington, IN. *Phi Delta Kappan.* (Fast back Series). Phi Delta Kappa International.

Banks, J. A. (1977c). Pluralism and educational concepts: A clarification. *Peabody Journal of Education, 54,* 73–78.

Banks, J. A. (1977d). A response to Phillip Freedman. *Phi Delta Kappan, 58,* 695–697.

Banks, J. A. (1978a). Ethnicity in contemporary American society:

Toward the development of a topology. *Ethnicity, 5,* 238–251.

Banks, J. A. (1978b). Multicultural education across cultures: United States, Mexico, Puerto Rico, France, and Great Britain. *Social Education, 42,* 177–185.

Banks, J. A. (1979a). Ethnicity: Implications for curriculum reform. *Social Studies, 70,* 3–10.

Banks, J. A. (1979b). Shaping the future of multicultural education. *Journal of Negro Education, 48,* 237–252.

Banks, J. A. (1980). Developing cross-cultural competency in the social studies. *Journal of Research and Development in Education, 13*(2), 113–122.

Banks, J. A. (1981). *Education in the 80s: Multiethnic education.* Washington, DC: National Education Association.

Banks, J. A. (1981a). Multiethnic curriculum: Goals and characteristics. In J. A. Banks (Ed.), *Education in the 80s: Multiethnic education.* Washington, DC: National Education Association.

Banks, J. A. (1981b). *Multiethnic education: Theory and practice.* Boston: Allyn and Bacon.

Banks, J. A. (1981c). The nature of multicultural education. In J. A. Banks (Ed.), *Education in the 80s: Multiethnic education.* Washington, DC: National Education Association.

Banks, J. A. (1981d). *Education in the 80s: Multiethnic education.* Washington, DC: National Education Association.

Banks, J. A. (1982a). Educating minority youths: An inventory of current theory. *Educating and Urban Society, 15,* 88–103.

Banks, J. A. (1982b). *We Americans: Our history and people.* Boston: Allyn & Bacon.

Banks, J. A. (1982c, March). *A study of Black suburban youths: Implications of the major findings for the Stages of Ethnicity typology.* Paper presented at the annual meeting of the American Research Association, New York. (ERIC Document Reproduction Service No. 226095).

Banks, J. A. (1983). Multiethnic education at the crossroads. *Phi Delta Kappan, 64,* 559.

Banks, J. A. (1983). The Presidential address: Cultural democracy, citizenship education, and the American dream. *Social Education, 47,* 178–232.

Banks, J. A. (1984a). *An exploratory study of assimilation, pluralism, and marginality: Black families in predominantly White suburbs.* Paper presented at the annual

Banks, J. A. (1984b). Black youths in predominantly White suburbs: An exploratory study of their attitudes and self-concepts. *Journal of Negro Education, 53,* 3–17.

Banks, J. A. (1984c). Values, ethnicity, social science research, and educational policy. In B. Ladner (Ed.), *The humanities in precollegiate education.* Chicago, IL: University of Chicago Press.

Banks, J. A. (1985a). Urban education: Educational programs. In T. Husen & T. Neville (Eds.), *International encyclopedia of education* (Vol. 9). Oxford, England: Pergmon.

Banks, J. A. (1985b). Ethnic revitalization movements and education. *Educational Review, 37,* 131–139.

Banks, J. A. (1985c). Multicultural education. In T. Husen & T. Neville (Eds.), *International encyclopedia of education* (Vol. 6). Oxford, England: Pergamon.

Banks, J. A. (1986a). Multicultural education and its critics: Britain and the United States. In S. Mogill, G. K. Verma, K. Mallick, & C. Mogdil (Eds.), *Multicultural education: The interminable debate.* London: Falmer.

Banks, J. A. (1986b). Race, ethnicity, and schooling in the United

States: Past, present, and future. In J. A. Banks & J. Lynch (Eds.), *Multicultural education in Western societies.* New York: Praeger.

Banks, J. A. (1987). The social studies, ethnic diversity, and social change. *Elementary School Journal, 87,* 531–543.

Banks, J. A. (1988a). Education, citizenship, and cultural options. *Education and Society, 1*(1), 19–22.

Banks, J. A. (1988b). Ethnicity, class, cognitive, and motivational styles: Research and teaching implications. *Journal of Negro Education, 57,* 452–466.

Banks, J. A. (1988c). *Multiethnic education: Theory and practice* (2nd ed.) Boston: Allyn and Bacon.

Banks, J. A. (Eds.). (1989a). *Multicultural education: Issues and perspectives.* Boston: Allyn & Bacon.

Banks, J. A. (1989b). Teaching for multicultural literacy. *Louisiana Social Studies Journal, 16*(1), 5–9.

Banks, J. A. (1989c). *Integrating the curriculum with ethnic content: Approaches and guidelines.* In J. A. Banks & C. A. M. Banks (Eds.), *Multicultural education: Issues and perspectives* (pp. 189–270). Boston, MA: Allyn and Bacon.

Banks, J. A. (1989d). *Multicultural education: Characteristics and goals.* In J. A. Banks & C. A. McGee Banks (Eds.), *Multicultural education: Issues and perspectives* (1st ed.) Boston: Allyn & Bacon.

Banks, J. A. (1990). Citizenship education for a pluralistic democratic society. *Social Studies, 81,* 210–214.

Banks, J. A. (1991a). A curriculum for empowerment, action and change. In C. E. Sleeter (Ed.), *Empowerment through multicultural education.* New York: State University of New York Press.

Banks, J. A. (1991b). *Curriculum guidelines for multicultural education.* Prepared by the NCSS Task force on Ethnic Studies Curriculum Guidelines. Washington, DC: National Education Association.

Banks, J. A. (1991c). Multicultural literacy and curriculum reform. *Educational Horizons, 69,* 135–140.

Banks, J. A. (1991d). *Multicultural education: Its effects on students' racial and gender role attitudes.* In J. P. Shaver (Ed.), *Handbook of research on social studies teaching and learning* (pp. 459–469). New York: Macmillan Publishers.

Banks, J. A. (1991e). Social studies, ethnic diversity, and social change. In C. V. Willie, A. M. Garbaldi, & W. L. Reed (Eds.), *The education of African Americans.* New York: Auburn House.

Banks, J. A. (1991). Teaching multicultural literacy to teachers. *Teaching Education, 4,* 135–144.

Banks, J. A. (1991g). *Teaching strategies for ethnic studies* (5th ed.). Boston: Allyn & Bacon.

Banks, J. A. (1992a). African American scholarship and the evolution of multicultural education. *The Journal of Negro Education, 61*(3), 273–286.

Banks, J. A. (1992b). It's up to us. *Teaching Tolerance, 1*(2), 20–23.

Banks, J. A. (1992c). Multicultural education and school reform. In D. Bragaw & W. S. Thompson (Eds.), *Multicultural education: A global approach.* New York: American Forum for Global Education.

Banks, J. A. (1992d). *Multicultural education for the 21st century.* Washington, DC: National Education Association.

Banks, J. A. (1992e). Multicultural education: Approaches,

developments, and dimensions. In J. Lynch, C. Mogdil, & S. Mogdil (Eds.), *Cultural diversity and the schools: Vol. 1: Education for cultural diversity: Convergence and divergence.* London: Falmer.

Banks, J. A. (1993a). The cannon, debate, knowledge construction, and multicultural education. *Educational Researcher, 22*(5), 4–14.

Banks, J. A. (1993b). Approaches to multicultural curriculum reform. In J. A. Banks & C. A. M. Banks (Eds.), *Multicultural education: Issues and perspectives* (2nd ed.). Boston: Allyn & Bacon.

Banks, J. A. (1993c). Multicultural education as an academic discipline. *Multicultural Education, 1*(3), 8–11, 39.

Banks, J. A. (1993d). Multicultural education for young children: Racial and ethnic attitudes and their modification. In B. Spodek (Ed.), *Handbook of research on the education of young children.* New York: Macmillan.

Banks, J. A. (1993e). Multicultural education: Characteristics and goals. In J. A. Banks & C. A. M. Banks (Eds.), *Multicultural education: Issues and perspectives* (2nd ed). Boston: Allyn & Bacon.

Banks, J. A. (1993f). Multicultural education: Development, dimensions, and challenges. *Phi Delta Kappan, 75,* 22–28.

Banks, J. A. (1993g). Multicultural education: Historical development, dimensions, and practice. In L. Darling-Hammond (Ed.), *Review of research in education 19.* Washington, DC: American Educational Research Association.

Banks, J. A. (1993h). Multicultural education: Progress and prospects. *Phi Delta Kappan, 75,* 21.

Banks, J. A. (1993i). The canon debate, knowledge construction, and multicultural education. *Educational Researcher, 22*(5), 4–114.

Banks, J. A. (1994a) Transforming the mainstream curriculum. *Educational Leadership, 51*(8), 4–8.

Banks, J. A. (1994b). *An introduction to multicultural education.* Boston: Allyn & Bacon.

Banks, J. A. (1994c). Multicultural education: Historical development, dimensions, and practice. In J. A. Banks & C. A. M. Banks (Eds.), *Handbook of research on the multicultural education.* New York: Macmillan.

Banks, J. A. (1994d). Transforming the mainstream curriculum. *Educational Leadership, 51*(8), 4–8

Banks, J. A. (1995a). Multicultural education: Its effects on students racial and gender role attitudes. In J. A. Banks (Ed.), *Handbook of research on multicultural education.* New York: Macmillan.

Banks, J. A. (1995b). The historical reconstruction of knowledge about race: Implications for transformative teaching. *Educational Researcher, 24*(2), 15–25.

Banks, J. A. (1996). *Multicultural education, transformative knowledge, and action: Historical and contemporary perspectives.* New York: Teachers College Press.

Banks, J. A. (1997). *Educating citizens in a multicultural society.* New York: Teachers College Press.

Banks, J. A. (1993). *Multicultural education for young children: Racial and ethnic attitude and their modification.* In B. Spodek (Ed.), *Handbook of research on the education of young children* (pp. 236–250). New York: Macmillan.

Banks, James A. (2006). Race, Culture, and Education. The Selected Works of James A. Banks. Routledge. Taylor Francis Group.

Banks, James A. (2006). Democracy and Diversity Princviples and Concepts for Educating Citizens in a Global Age: CME Publications. Seattle, Washington.

Banks, Cherry A. McGee. (2006). Improving Multicultural Education. Teachers College Press. New York. NY.

Banks, J. A. (1994). *An introduction to multicultural education.* Boston: Allyn and Bacon.

Banks, J. A. (1995). The historical reconstruction of knowledge about race: Implications for transformative teaching. *Educational Researcher, 24*(2), 15–25.

Banks, J. A. (1999). *Educating citizens in a multicultural society.* New York: Teachers College Press.

Banks, J. A. (2001). *Cultural diversity and education: Foundations, curriculum, and teaching.* Needham Heights, MA: Allyn and Bacon.

Banks, J. A. (Eds.). (1989). *Multicultural education: Issues and perspectives.* Boston: Allyn & Bacon.

Banks, J. A. (February, 1982). *Reducing prejudice in students: Theory, research, and strategies.* Paper presented in the Kamloops Spring Institute for teacher Education Lecture Series. Buraby, British Columbia, Canada. (ERIC Document Reproduction service No. ED215930).

Banks, J. A. (March, 1986). *Cultural diversity in western societies: Challenges and opportunities.* Paper presented at the annual meeting of the Association of Supervision and Curriculum Development, San Francisco. (ERIC Document Reproduction Service ED274577).

Banks, J. A. (September, 1981). *Social problems and educational equity in the eighties.* Paper presented at a working meeting of the School Finance Project, United States Department of Education, Washington, DC. (ERIC Document Reproduction Service No. ED220336).

Banks, J.A., & Banks, C.A.M. (1993). *Multicultural education: Issues and perspectives* (2nd ed.). Boston, MA: Allyn and Bacon.

Banks, J.A., & Banks, C. M. (1995). Social studies teacher education, ethnic diversity, and academic achievement. *International Journal of Social Education, 7*(3), 24– 38.

Banks, J. A., & Clegg, A., Jr. (1990). *Teaching strategies for the social studies: Inquiry, valuing, and decision-making* (4th ed.). New York: Longman.

Banks, J. A., Cortes, C.E., Gay, G., Garcia, R.L., & Ochoa, A.S. (1992). *Curriculum guidelines for multicultural education. A position statement of the National Council for Social Studies* (Revised edition). Washington, DC: *National Council for Social Studies.*

Banks, J. A., Darling-Hammond, D., & Greene, M. (1992). *Building learning centered schools: Three perspectives.* New York: Teachers College Press.

Banks, J.A. & Banks, C.A.M. (2004). Handbook of Multicultural Education (Second Edition). Jossey-Bass. San Francisco, Calif. John Wiley and Sons.

Bell, D. (1973). *Race, racism and American law.* Boston, MA: Little Brown.

Ben-Johannan, Y. (1972). *Cultural genocide in the Black and African studies curriculum.* New York: Alkebu-Lan.

Bennett, C. L. (1995). *Comprehensive multicultural educa-*

tion: Theory and practice (3rd ed.). Boston, MA: Allyn & Bacon.

Bennett, L. (1975). The Shaping of Black America. The Struggles and Triumphs of African-Americans, 1619 to the 1990's. (Author of Before the Mayflower). Penguin Press. Johnson Publishing. New York. (Reprinted: 1969, 1971, 1972, 1973, 1974, 1975).

Bennett, L. (1962). *Before the Mayflower: A history of Black America.* Chicago, IL: Johnson Publishing Co.

Bernal, M. (1987). *Black Athena Greece.* London: Free Association Press.

Bloom, A. (1987). *The closing of the American mind.* New York: Simon & Schuster.

Blyden, E. W. (1971). *Christianity, Islam and the Negro race* (1887). Edinboro, Scotland: University Press.

Bond, H. M. (1939). *Negro education in Alabama: A study in cotton and steel.* Washington, DC: The Associated Publishers.

Booth, W. C., Colomb, G. G., & Williams, J. M. (1995). *The craft of research.* Chicago: University of Chicago Press.

Branch, T. (1988). *Parting the waters: America in the King years.* New York: Simon and Schuster.

Britzman, D. P. (1991). *Practice makes practice: A critical study of learning to teach.* Albany, NY: SUNY Press.

Brown v. Board of Education of Topeka, Kansas. (1954). 347 U.S. 483 (152, 151).

Carby, H. V. (1992). *Black popular culture: Multicultural wars.* Seattle, WA: Bay Press.

Carson, D., & Freidman, L. D. (1995). *Shared differences: Multicultural media and practical pedagogy.* Chicago: University of Illinois Press.

Casara, B. A. (1990). *Adult education in a multicultural society:* New York: Routledge.

Chinn, P. C. (1985). Language as a function of culture. *Social Education, 48*(5), 101– 103.

Chinn, P., & Gollnick, D. (1990). *Multicultural education in a pluralistic society* (3rd ed.). New York: Merrill.

Chinweizu. (1987). *Decolonizing the African mind.* London, England: Pero Press.

Chou, V., Watkins, W. H., Lewis, J. H. (2001). *Race and education: The roles of history and society in educating African American students.* Boston, MA: Allyn and Bacon.

Churchill, W. (1992). *Fantasies of the master race. Literature, cinema and the colonialization of American Indians.* Monroe, ME: Common Courage Press.

Clark, C., & O'Donnell, J. (1999). *Owning and disowning a racial identity: Becoming and unbecoming White.* Critical Studies in Education and Culture Series. Westport, CT: Bergin and Garvey.

Clark, J. H. (1991). *Africans at the crossroad: Notes for an African world revolution.* Trenton, NJ: African World Press.

Clayton, C., & Potter, J. (1994). *African American firsts: Famous, little known and unsung triumphs of Blacks in America.* Elizabethtown, NY: Pinto Press.

Colangelo, N., Dustin, D., & Foxley, C.H. (Eds.). (1985). *Multicultural non-sexist education: A human relations approach.* Dubuque, IA. Kendall/Hunt.

Cole, D. (1999). *No equal justice: Race and class in the American criminal justice system.* New York: New Press.

Cook, D. R., & LaFluer, K. N. (1975). A guide to educational research (2nd ed.) Boston: Allyn and Bacon.

Cook, L. A. (1951). *Intergroup relations in teacher education* (College Study in Intergroup Education, volume II). Washington, DC: American Council on Education.

Cortes, C. E. (1995, 1973). Teaching the Chicano experience. In J. A. Banks (Ed.), *Teaching ethnic studies: Concepts, and strategies* (*43rd Yearbook*) (pp. 181–199). Washington, DC: National Council for the Social Studies.

Cortes, C. E. (2002). *The making and remaking of a multiculturalist.* (James Banks, Editor). New York: Teachers College Press.

Cross, D. E., Baker, G. C., & Stiles, L. J. (Eds.) (1977). *Teaching in a multicultural society: Perspectives and professional strategies.* New York: The Free Press.

Cruse, H. (1967). *The crisis of the Negro intellectual.* New York: William Morrow and Co., Inc.

Davidman, L., & Davidman, P. T. (1994/1997/2001). *Teaching with a multicultural perspective: A practical guide.* (3rd ed.). New York: Allyn and Bacon.

D'Sousa, D. (1996). *Illiberal education.* Riverside, NJ: Simon and Schuster Trade.

Derman-Sparks, L., & the ABC Task Force. (1989). *Anti bias curriculum: Tools for empowering young children*

DeGraft-Johnson, J. C. (1986). *African glory: The story of vanished Negro civilizations (first publication date, 1954).* Baltimore, MD: Black Classic Press.

Dilg, M. A. (1999). *Race and culture in the classroom: Teaching and learning through multicultural education. New York: Teachers College Press.*

Diop, C. A. (1974). *The African origin of civilization: Myth or reality.* Westport, CT: Lawrence Hill and Co.

Diop, C. A. (1978). *The cultural unity of Black Africa: The*

domains of patriarchy and matriarchy in classical antiquity.
Chicago, IL: Third World Press.

Diop, C. A. (1991). *Civilization or barbarism: An authentic anthropology.* Westport, CT: Lawrence Hill Books.

Drake, St. C. (1987). Black folk here and there: An essay in history and anthropology (Volume I). Los Angeles: Center for Afro-American Studies, University of California.

DuBois, W.E.B. (1935). Black reconstruction in America: An essay toward a history of the part which Black folk played in the attempt to reconstruct democracy in America, 1860–1880. New York: Harcourt Brace & Co.

DuBois. W.E.B. (1947). The world and Africa: An inquiry into the part which Africa has played in world history. New York: Viking Press.

DuBois, W.E.B. (1969) *The souls of Black folk.* New York: Signet Classic.

DuBois, W.E.B. (1973/1903). *The souls of Black folks.* Greenwich, CT: Fawcett Press.

Dyson, M. E. (1996). *Race rules: Navigating the color line.* Reading, MA: Addison Wesley.

The Education for All Handicapped Children Act of 1975. Public Law 94-142.

Fanon, F. (1967). *Black skin, White masks.* New York: Grove Press.

Farmer, Edgar I., Rojewski, Jay, and Farmer, Barbara. (2003). Diversity in America : Visions ofthe Future. Real Issues of Real People. Kendall Publishing Co. Dubuque, Iowa.

Forbes, J. D. (1973). *Teaching Native American values and cultures.* In J. A. Banks (Ed.), *Teaching ethnic studies: Concepts and strategies (43rd Yearbook)* (pp. 201–225). Washington, DC: National Council for the Social Studies.

Forbs, J. (1989). *Black Africans and Native Americans: Color, race and cast in the evolution of Red-African people.* London, England: Blackwell Press.

Foreman, G. (1977). *The five civilized tribes.* Norman, OK.

Frankenberg, R. (1993). *The social construction of Whiteness: White women, race matters.* Minneapolis, MN: University of Minnesota Press.

Franklin, J. H. (1985). *George Washington Williams: A biography.* Chicago: The University of Chicago Press.

Franklin, J. H. (1990). *Race and history: Selected essays.* Baton Rouge: Louisiana State University Press.

Franklin, J. H., & Moss, A. A., Jr. (1988). *From slavery to freedom: A history of Negro Americans* (6th ed.). New York: Alfred A. Knopf.

Freire, P. (1970). *Pedagogy of the oppressed.* New York. Seabury Press.

Fulani, L. (1988). *The psychopathology of everyday racism and sexism.* New York: Harrington Park Press.

Garvey, A. J. (1970). *Garvey and Garveyism.* New York: Collier Macmillan.

Gay, G. (1985). Implications for selected models of ethnic identity development for educators. *Journal of Negro Education, 54,* 43–55.

Gay, G. (1995a). The state of multicultural education in the United States. In K. Adams-Moodley (Ed.), *Education in plural societies: International perspectives.* Calgary: Detselig.

Gay, G. (1995b). Bridging multicultural theory and practice. *Multicultural Education, 3*(1), 4–9.

Gay, G. (1995c). Mirror images on common issues: Parallels between multicultural education and critical pedagogy.

In C. Sleeter & P. McClaren (Eds.), *Multicultural education, critical pedagogy, and the politics of difference* (pp. 155–189). Albany: State University of New York Press.

Gay, G., & Baber, W. L. (Eds.). (1987). *Expressively Black: The cultural basis of ethnic identity.* New York: Praeger.

Gibbs, J. T. (Ed.) (1988). *Young, Black and male in America: An endangered species.* Dover, MA: Auburn House.

Gibson, M. A. (1988). *Accommodation without assimilation: Sikh immigrants in an American high school.* Ithaca, NY: Cornell University Press.

Gibson, M. A. (1988). The school performance of immigrant minorities: A comparative view. *Anthropology and Education Quarterly, 18*, 262–275.

Giddings, J. (1964). The exiles of Florida: Or the crimes committed by our government against the maroons, who fled from South Carolina and other slave states, seeking protection under Spanish laws (1858). Gainesville, FL: University of Florida Press.

Gillborn, D. (1995). *Racism and anti-racism in real schools.* Bristol, PA: Open University Press.

Gilroy, P. (1993). *The Black Atlantic: Modernity and double consciousness.* Cambridge, MA: Harvard University Press.

Giroux, H. A. (1983). Theory and resistance to education: A pedagogy for the opposition. Hadley, MA: Bergin and Garvey.

Giroux, H. A. (1988). Teachers as intellectuals: Toward a critical pedagogy of learning. New York: Bergin and Garvey.

Giroux, H. A. (1989). *Critical pedagogy: The state and cultural struggle.* Albany, NY: SUNY Press.

Giroux, H. A. (1996). *Fugitive cultures.* New York: Routledge Press.

Giroux, H. A., Lankshear, C., McLaren, P., & Peters, M. (1996). *Counternarratives: Cultural studies and critical pedagogues on postmodern spaces.* New York: Routledge Press.

Gollnick, D., & Chinn, P. (2001, 1995, 1990, 1986). *Multicultural education in a pluralistic society.* New York: Macmillan.

Graff, G. (1992). *Beyond the cultural wars: How teaching the conflicts can revitalize American education.* New York: W.W. Norton Press.

Grant, C. A. (1977). *Multicultural education: Commitments, issues, and applications.* Washington, DC: Association for Supervision and Curriculum Development.

Grant, C. A. (1995). *Educating for diversity: An anthology of multicultural voices.* Boston, MA: Allyn and Bacon.

Grant, C. A., & Ladson-Billings, G. (1997). *Dictionary of multicultural education.* Phoenix, AZ: Oryx Press.

Grant, C. A., & Sleeter, C. (1988). *Making choices for multicultural education: Five approaches to race, class, and gender.* New York: Macmillan.

Green, M. (1988). *The dialectics of freedom.* New York: Teachers College Press.

Gresson, A. D. III., Steinberg, S., & Kincheloe, J. (1994). *Measured lies.* Minneapolis, MN: Minnesota Press.

Guba, E. & Lincoln, Y. (1988). *Naturalistic inquiry.* Newbury Park, CA: Sage.

Guralnick, D. B. (Ed.) (1980). *Webster's new world dictionary of the American language* (2nd ed.). New York: Simon and Schuster.

Hacker, A. (1992). *Two nations: Black and White, separate, hostile, unequal.* New York. Ballantine.

Haddad, D. B. (1995). *Multicultural education: The views of three contemporary African American Theorists: James A. Banks, Carl A. Grant, and Asa Hilliard III.* South Carolina: University of South Carolina (Library).

Hadjor, K. B. (1993) *Another America; The politics of race and blame.* Boston: South End Press.

Harding, V. (1981). *There is a river: The Black struggle for freedom in America.* New York: Vintage Books.

Harris, J. E. (Ed.). (1974). *Pillars in Ethiopian history: The William Leo Hansberry African history notebook.* Washington, DC: Howard University Press.

Harris, J. E. (1977). *Africa and Africans as seen by classical writers: The William Leo Hansberry African history notebook* (Vol. 2). Washington, DC: Howard University Press.

Heath, S. B. (1983). *Ways with words: Language, life, and work in communities and classrooms.* New York: Cambridge University Press.

Herskovits, M. J. (1958). *The myth of the Negro past.* Boston: Beacon Press.

Helms, J. E. (1990). *Black and White racial identity: Toward a theory, research, and practice.* Westport, CT: Greenwood Press.

Higginbottom, A. L. (1978). *In the matter of color: Race and the American legal process.* New York: Oxford University Press.

Hilliard, A. G., Payton-Stewart, L., & Williams, L. O. (1990). *The infusion of African and African American content in the school curriculum.* First National Conference Proceedings, October 1989. New Jersey: Aaron Press.

Hilliard, A., III. (1993). *50 essential references on the history of African people.* Baltimore, MD: Black Classic Press.

Hilliard, A., III. (1994). *The maroon within us.* Baltimore, MD: Black Classic Press.

Hillis, M. R. (1995) Allison Davis and the study of race, social class and schooling. The *Journal of Negro Education, 64*(1), 33–41.

Hine, D. C. (1993). *Black women in America: An historical encyclopedia.* Brooklyn, NY: Carlson Publishing, Inc. (Editors E. Barkley Brown and R. Terborg-Penn)

Hirsch, E. D., Jr. (1987). *Cultural literacy: What every American needs to know.* Boston: Houghton Mifflin.

Hirsch, E. D., Jr. (1996a). *The first dictionary of cultural literacy.* Boston: Houghton Mifflin.

Hirsch, E. D., Jr. (1996b). *The schools we need: Why we don't have them?* New York: Doubleday.

Holtzclaw, R. F. (1980). *The saints go marching in: A one-volume hagiography of Africans, or descendents of Africans who have been canonized by the church including three of the early popes.* Shaker Heights, OH: The Keeple Press, Inc.

hooks, b. (1981). *Ain' t I a Women: Black women feminism.* Boston, MA: South End Press.

hooks, b. (1984). *Feminist theory from margin to center.* Boston, MA: South End Press.

hooks, b. (1989). *Talking back: thinking feminism, thinking Black.* Boston, MA: South End Press.

hooks, b. (1990). *Yearning: Race, gender, and cultural politics.* Boston, MA: South End Press.

Hoskins, L. A. (1990). Decoding European geopolitics: Afrocentric perspectives. African American Affairs. Monographic Series, vol. 4, no. 2. The Institute for African

American Affairs, Kent State University, Kent, OH.

Houston, D. D. (1985 reprint). *Wonderful Ethiopians of the ancient Cushite empire (1926)*. Baltimore, MD: Black Classic Press.

Howard, G. R. (1993). Whites in multicultural education: Rethinking our role. Phi Delta Kappan, 75(12), 36–41.

Howard, G. R. (1999). We can't teach what we don't know: White teachers, multicultural schools. New York: Teachers College Press.

Huberman, M. A., & Miles, M. B. (1984). Qualitative data analysis: Sourcebook of new methods. Newbury Park, CA: Sage.

Jabbar, K. A. (1996). *Black profiles in courage: A legacy of African American achievement.* New York: William Morrow.

Jackson, J. (1972). *Man, God, and civilization.* New York: University Books.

Jacoby, R. (1994). Dogmatic wisdom: How the culture wars divert education and distract America. New York: Doubleday.

James, G. G. M. (1954). *Stolen legacy.* San Francisco, CA: Julian Richardson.

Johnson, E. A. (1891). *A history of the Negro race in America: From 1619 to 1880: The origin of the race. Short Sketch of Liberia.* New York: Edwards & Broughton Printers and Binders.

Johnson, E. A. (1893). (revised edition). A school history of the Negro race in America from 1619 to 1880. The Origin of the Race. New York: W.L. Conkey and Printers.

Johnson, E. A. (1904). *Light ahead for the Negro.* New York: W.L. Conkey Printers.

Josephy, Jr., A. M. (1991). *The Indian heritage of America.* New York: Houghton Mifflin Co.

Kallen, H. M. (1956). *Cultural pluralism and the American idea.* Philadelphia: University of Pennsylvania Press.

Katz, W. L. (1973). *Black people who made the Old West.* New York.

Katz, W. L. (1986). *Black Indians: A hidden heritage.* New York: Macmillan Publishing Co.

Katz, W. L. (1987). The Black west: A pictorial history (3rd ed.). Seattle, WA: Open Hand Publishing.

Katz, W. L. (1974). Teachers guide to American Negro history. New York: New View Points.

Katz, W. L. (1986). *Black Indians: A hidden heritage.* New York: Atheneum/Macmillan.

Kettering Foundation. (2000). *Racial and ethnic tensions: What should we do?* Washington, DC: National Public Issues Forum Institute.

Kincheloe, J. L. & Steinberg, S. R. (1997). *Changing multiculturalism.* Philadelphia: Open University Press.

Kincheloe, J. L., Steinberg, S. R., Rodriguez, N. M., & Chennault, R. E. (1998). *White reign: Deploying Whiteness in America.* New York: St. Martin's Press:

King, J., & Mitchell, C.A. (1995). *Black mothers to sons: Juxtaposing African American literature with special practice* (Revised). New York: Peter Lang.

King, K. (1971). *Pan Africanism and education: A study of race philanthropy and education in the southern states of America and East Africa.* Oxford, England: Clarendon Press.

Kozol, J. (1981). *Savage inequalities: Children in America's schools.* New York: Crown.

Ladson Billings, G. (1994). *The Dreamkeepers: Successful teachers of African American children.* San Francisco, CA: Jossey–Bass.

Lane–Poole, S. (1990). *The story of the Moors in Spain (1886)*. Baltimore, MD: Black Classic Press.

Lawrence, W., & Sachar, A. L. (1973). *A history of the Jews* (5th ed.). New York: Knopf.

Leckie, W. H. (1967). *The buffalo soldiers: A narrative of the Negro calvary in the West*. Norman, OK: University of Oklahoma Press.

Lee, E., Menkart, D., & Okazawa, M. (Eds.) (1998). *Beyond heroes and holidays: A practical guide to K–12 anti-racist, multicultural education and staff development*. Washington, DC: Network of Educators on the Americas.

Lefkowitz, M. (1996). *Not out of Africa: How Afrocentrism became an excuse to teach myth as history*. New York: Harper Collins, Basic Books.

Lewis, D. L. (1987). The *race to Fashoda: European colonialism and African resistance in the scramble for Africa*. New York: Weidenfeld and Nicolson.

Litwack, L. (1979). *Been in the storm so long: The aftermath of slavery*. New York: Vintage.

Lockwood, A. T. (1994). Whose Unum? *Focus in Change, 16,* 12–14.

Loewen, J.W. (1995). *Lies my teacher told me: Everything your American history textbook got wrong*. New York: Touchstone Books/Simon & Schuster.

Logan, R. W., & Winston, M. R. (Eds.). (1982). *Dictionary of American Negro biography*. New York: W.W. Norton.

Lynman, S. M. (1972). *The Black American in sociological thought: A failure of perspective*. New York: Capricorn Books.

MacRitchie, D. (1986). *Ancient and modern Britons. 2 vols.* Los Angeles, CA: William Preston.

Massey, G. (1974). *Book of the beginnings: Containing an attempt to recover and reconstitute the lost origins of the myths and mysteries, types, and symbols, religion and language, with Egypt as the mouthpiece and Africa as the birthplace, 2 Vols.* Secaucus, NJ: University Books, Inc.

Mazel, E. (1998). *"And don't call me a racist!" A treasury of quotes on the past, present, and future of the color line in America.* Lexington, MA: Argonaut Press.

McLaren, P., & Giroux, H. (1997). *Between borders: Pedagogy and the politics of cultural studies.* New York: Routledge.

Meier, A., & Rudwick, E. (1986). *Black history and the historical profession, 1915–1980.* Urbana, IL: University of Illinois Press.

Meriam, S. B. (1991). *Case study research in education: A qualitative approach.* San Francisco: Jossey–Bass.

Meyers, L. J. (1988). *Understanding the Afrocentric world view.* Dubuque, IA: Kendall/Hunt.

Myers, S. L., Jr., & Turner, C. S. V. (2000). Faculty of color in academe: Bittersweet success. New York: Allyn and Bacon.

NAACP. (1939). *Anti-Negro propaganda in school textbooks.* New York: Author.

Nash, G. B. (1992). *Red, White, and Black: The peoples of early North America.* Englewood Cliffs, NJ: Simon and Schuster.

NCATE. (Revised: 2000, 1979, 1977). National Council for Accreditation of Teacher Educators. Multicultural Education (2.1) Standards. (May 11, 2000) www.ncate. org.

Nieto, S. (1992). *Affirming diversity: The socio–political context of multicultural education.* White Plains, NY: Longman Press.

Nieto, S. (1999). The light in their eyes. Creating multicultural learning communities. New York: Teachers College Press.

Novak, M. (1971). *The rise of the unmeltable ethnics.* New York: Macmillan.

O Hearn, C. C. (1998). Half and half Writers on growing up bi–racial and b–cultural. New York: Pantheon.

Obenga, T. (1992). *Ancient Egypt and Black Africa: A student's handbook for the study of ancient Egypt in philosophy, linguistics and gender relations.* London: Karnak House.

Ogbu, J. (1988). Class stratification, racial stratification, and schooling. In L. Weiss (Ed.), Class, race, and gender in American education (pp. 163–182). Albany: State University of New York Press.

Okihiro, G. Y. (1994). Margins and mainstreams: Asians in American history and culture. Seattle: University of Washington Press.

Omi, M., & Winant, H. (1986). Racial formation in the United States: From the 1960s to the 1990s. New York: Routledge.

Parker, G. W. (1917). African origin of Grecian civilization. Journal of Negro History, 2(3), 334–344.

Pate, A. (1997). *Amistad.* New York: Signet/Penguin Group.

Patton, M. Q. (1990). Qualitative evaluation and research methods (2nd ed.) Newbury Park, CA: Sage.

Pearlman, J. (1988). *Interdisciplinary perspectives on modern history: Ethnic differences on schooling and social structure among the Irish, Italians, Jews, and Blacks in an American city (1880–1935).* Cambridge, England: Cambridge University Press.

Pine, G. J., & Hilliard, A. G. III. (1990). Rx for racism:

Imperative for America s schools. Phi Delta Kappan, 71, 593–599.

Platt, A. M. (1991). E. Franklin Frazier reconsidered. New Brunswick, NJ: Rutgers University Press.

Portland Public Schools. (1987). African American baseline essays. Portland, OR: Multinomah School District 1J.

Price, R. (Ed.). (1973). *Maroon societies: Rebel slave communities in the Americas.* New York: Anchor Books.

Ravitch, D. (1990). Multiculturalism: E Pluribus Plures. *American Scholar, 59*(3), 337– 354.

Ravitch, D., & Finn, C. C. (1987). What do our seventeen year olds know? New York: Harper and Row.

Reisman, F. (1962). *The culturally deprived child.* New York: Harper and Row.

Reisman, F. (1976). *The inner city child.* New York: Harper and Row.

Roediger, D. R. (1991). The wages of Whiteness: Race and the making of the American working class. New York: Verso.

Rogers, J. A. (1952). Nature knows no color line: Research into Negro ancestry in the White race. St. Petersburg, FL: Helga M. Rodgers.

Romo, H. (2000). *Multicultural annual.* 7th ed. Akron, OH: McGraw–Hill.

Romo, Harriet D. (Spring 2000). Improving Ethnic and Racial Relations in the Schools, Eric Review.

Root, M. P. (1992). *Racially mixed people in America.* Newbury Park, CA: Sage Publications.

Rutherford, J. (1990). *Identity: Community, culture, and difference.* North Wales.

Ryan, W. (1971). *Blaming the victim.* New York.

Saad, E. N. (1983). *The social history of Timbuctoo: The role of Muslim scholars and notables, 1400–1900.* New York: Cambridge University Press.

Schlesinger, A. M., Jr. (1998, 1991). The disuniting of America: Reflections on a multicultural society. The Larger Agenda Series. Nashville, TN: Whittle Direct Books.

Shipley, D. (1997). *A country of strangers: Blacks in America.* New York: Alfred Knopf.

Shoat, E., & Stam, R. (1994, 1995, 1996). *Unthinking eurocentrism: Multiculturalism and the media.* New York: Routledge.

Shorris, E. (1992). *Latinos: A biography of the people.* New York: Avon Books.

Sleeter, C. E. (1989). Multicultural education as a form of resistance to oppression. *Journal of Education, 171,* 51–71.

Sleeter, C. E. (1994). White racism. *Multicultural education, 1*(4), 5–8, 39.

Sleeter, C. E. & Grant, C. A. (1999, 1995, 1991, 1988). Making choices for multicultural education: Five approaches to race, class, and gender. Columbus, OH: Merrill. (3rd ed., Wiley).

Sleeter, C. E., & McLaren, P. L. (1995). Introduction: Exploring connections to build a critical multiculturalism. In C. Sleeter & P. McClaren (Eds.), Multicultural education, critical pedagogy, and the politics of difference (pp. 1–32). Albany: State University of New York Press.

Smith, G. P. (1998). Common sense about uncommon knowledge: The knowledge bases for diversity. Washington, DC: AACTE.

Sowell, T. (Ed.) (1986). Education: Assumptions versus history. Stanford, CA: Hoover Institute Press.

Spivey, D. (1978). Schooling for the new slavery: Black industrial education, 1868–1915. Westport, CT: Greenwood Press.

Stam, R., & Shohat, E. (1995). Unthinking eurocentrism: Multiculturalism and the media (2nd ed.) New York: Routledge.

Stamp, K. M. (1956). *The peculiar institution.* New York: Random House.

Staples, R. (1982). Black masculinity: The Black male's role in American society. San Francisco: Black Scholar Press.

Steele, S. (1991). Content of our character: A new vision of race in America. New York: Harper–Collins.

Stewart, J. (1998*). A framework to foster diversity at Penn State: 1998–2003.* University Park, PA: The Pennsylvania State University.

Suzuki, B. H. (1989, November/December). Asian Americans as the model minority. Change Magazine.

Suzuki, R. (1985). Curriculum transformation for multicultural education. Education and Urban Society, 16(3), 294–322.

Swartz, W. (1999). The identity Development of Multicracial Youth. Eric/Cue. Digest, No. 137, Eric Clearinhouse on Urban Education, New York, NY. (ED425248).

Taba, H, Brady, E. H., & Robinson, J. T. (1952). *Intergroup education in public schools.* Washington, DC: American Council on Education.

Taba, H., & Elkins, D. (1966). Teaching strategies for the culturally disadvantaged. Chicago: Rand McNally.

Taba, H., & Wilson, H.E. (1946). Intergroup education through the school curriculum. *Annals of the American Academy of Political and Social Science, 244,* 19–25.

Takaki, R. (1979). *Iron cages: Race and culture in the 19th Century in America.* New York: Oxford University Press.

Takaki, R. (1987). *Strangers from a different shore: A history of Asian Americans.* New York: Penguin Books Press.

Takaki, R. (1993). *A different mirror: A history of multicultural America.* Boston, MA: Little, Brown, Inc.

Takaki, R. (1995). *Violence in the black imagination: Essays and documents.* New York: Oxford University Press.

Talty, S. (2003). *Mulatto America: At the crossroads of Black and White culture: A social history.* New York. Harper Collins Publishers.

Tan, A. (1989). *The joy luck club.* New York: Putnam Publishing Group.

Temple, R. K. G. (1976). *The Sirius mystery.* New York: St. Martin's Press.

Terkel, S. (1991, September 2). The challenge of diversity: Ethnic groups change names with the times. *San Francisco Examiner.*

Terkel, S. (1995). (1992). *Race: How Blacks and Whites think and feel about the American obsession.* New York: The New Press.

Thernstrom, A., & Stephen, A. (1997). *America in Black and White: One nation indivisible.* Riverside, NH: Simon and Schuster Trade.

Thomas. Q. B. (1964). *The Negro in the making of America.* New York: Macmillan.

Tiedt, Iris M. & Tiedt, Pamela L. (Sixth Edition). (2002). Multicultural Teaching: a handbook of Activities, Information, and Resources. Allyn & Bacon. New York. (Revised 1999, 1995, 1986, 19790. Boston, Massachusetts.

Trent, J. S. (1995). *Notes of a White Black woman: Race, color, and community.* University Park, PA: The Pennsylvania State University.

Trotter, J. W., Jr., & Smith, E. L. (1997). *African Americans in Pennsylvania: Shifting historical perspectives.* University Park, PA: The Pennsylvania State University.

Tuckman, B. W. (1972). *Conducting educational research.* New York: Harcourt Brace Jovanovich.

Ukpokodu, O. (2003). Teaching multicultural education from a critical perspective: Challenges and dilemma. *Multicultural Perspectives Magazine, 5*(4), 17–23.

United States Congress, Senate, Committee on Indian Affairs. (1993). The Five Nations Citizens Land Reform Act was changed to the Five Civilized Tribes (HR2880)(Cherokee, Seminoles, Creek, Chickasaw, Choctaw). September 18, 2002. Washington, DC.

UNESCO. (1981). *General history of Africa.* Berkeley, CA: University of California Press.

Van Maanen, J. (1988). *Tales of the field: On writing ethnography.* Chicago, IL: University of Chicago Press.

Van Sertima, I. (1976). *They came before Columbus.* New York: Random House.

Van Sertima, I. (1985). *Journal of African civilizations: African presence in early Europe.* New Brunswick, NJ: Transaction Press.

Van Sertima, I. (1989). *Journal of African civilizations: Egypt revisited.* New Brunswick, NJ: Transaction Press.

Van Sertima, I. (1991). *Golden age of the Moor*. New Brunswick, NJ: Transaction Press.

Van Sertima, I., & Rashidi, R. (Eds.). (1988). *Journal of African civilizations: African presence in early Asia*. New Brunswick, NJ: Transaction Press.

Van Sertima, I., & Williams, L. (Eds). (1989). *Journal of African civilizations: Great African thinkers: Cheikh Anta Diop*. New Brunswick, NJ: Transaction Press.

Wa Thiong'o, N. (1987). *Decolonizing the mind: The politics of language in African literature*. London, England: James Currey.

Walden, D. (1970). *On being Black*. Greenwich, CT: Fawcett.

Washburn, D. E, Brown, N. L. & Abbott, R. W. (1996). *Multicultural education in the United States*. Philadelphia, PA: Inquiry International.

Wesley, C. H. (1969). *Richard Allen: Apostle of freedom*. Washington, DC: The Associated Publishers (Original work published in 1935).

West, C. (1993). *Race matters*. Boston: Beacon Press.

West, C., & Gates, H. L. (1997). *The future of the race*. New York: Random House, Value.

White W. F. (1929). *Rope and fagott: A biography of Judge Lynch*. New York: Alfred A. Knopf, Inc.

White, W. (1939). *Anti Negro propaganda in school textbooks*. (NAACP). New York.

White, W. F. (1924). *Fire in the flint*. New York: Alfred A. Knopf, Inc.

White, W. F. (1926). *Flight. White*. New York: Alfred A. Knopf, Inc.

Williams, C. (1974). *The destruction of Black civilization: Great issues of a race from 4,000 BC to 2,000 AD.* Chicago, IL: Third World Press.

Williams, G. W. (1989). *History of the Negro race in America from 1619–1880: Negroes as slaves, as soldiers, and as citizens (2 vols.).* Salem, NH: Ayer. (Original works published in 1882 and 1883).

Wilson, A. (1990). *Black on Black violence: The psychodynamics of Black self annihilation in service of White domination.* New York: African World Systems.

Wilson, W. J. (1978). *The declining significance of race: Blacks and changing American institutions.* Chicago: University of Chicago Press.

Woodson, C. G. (1933). *The mis–education of the Negro.* Washington, DC: The Associated Publishers.

Yette, S. (1971). *The choice: The issue of Black survival in America.* Silver Spring, MD: Cottage Books.

Zinn, H. (1980). *A people's history of the United States.* New York. Harper Colophon.

Survey Research Instrument

Multicultural Education Pilot Study Survey (MEPSS)

Date_____

Dear Survey Participants,

I believe that students receiving more information on multicultural education issues in pre–service teacher training will be more knowledgeable about multicultural education than students who have not received any training in multicultural education issues of diversity. As part of my research on developing a strategy for creating and designing a multicultural education curriculum intervention in pre–

service teacher training in the College of Education, I would like to know if students feel they have an opportunity to receive adequate knowledge of multicultural education and if their attitude towards multicultural education is positive or negative. I would like to have students in the College of Education consider their awareness and knowledge of multicultural education issues. I will select students in Psychology 002, Early Childhood Education, Language and Literacy and Curriculum and Instruction Courses, to complete the following survey to determine students perceptions of the need for multicultural courses on diversity issues. The survey consists of 15 statements. A pilot multicultural education diversity course will be designed and offered after the study is approved and completed. I would appreciate your participation.

Thank you for your participation and cooperation in this survey.

Sincerely,

Andrew Jackson, Sr.

Directions

Please rate your responses on a scale of 1 to 5 where 1=strongly disagree, 2=disagree, 3=undecided, unsure, or neutral, 4=agree, and 5=strongly agree.

(1) I have adequate understanding of multicultural education._____

(2) I have had more than one diversity or multicultural education course._____

(3) I feel Race influences your teaching style.____

(4) I feel that gender influences your teaching style.___

(5) I feel that ethnicity influences your teaching style.__

(6) I feel that social–economic class influences your teaching style._____

(7) I feel that faculty have a sincere interest in the inclusion of multicultural education and diversity in the curriculum.____

(8) I feel that diversity courses enhance your knowledge and understanding of multicultural education.____

(9) I have had at least one course on multicultural education available as part of my curriculum.____

(10) I would be willing to take an additional course to discuss and learn about diversity issues.____

(11) I feel there are adequate books, films, articles, and educational resources available to me in the library on multicultural education._____

(12) I feel students are being prepared to face the cross cultural challenges of the New Millenium and the 21st Century._____

(13) I feel that White students are uncomfortable teaching ethnic minorities and People of Color._____

(14) I feel Students of Color are uncomfortable teaching White students.___

(15) I feel students have an opportunity for cross cultural interaction in their classes._____

Demographic information:: (Please make a check mark or fill in a response to the following items that pertain to you): additional comments are welcome on the back of the survey instrument.

Male_____ Female_____ (check one) Ethnicity_____ (describe or fill in)

1st year student_____ Sophomore ____ Junior ____Senior ____ Race____ Age___

Number of Diversity Courses Completed_____ Major___

Please return all completed survey instruments to:
Andrew Jackson, Sr.
Penn State University
College of Education

228 Chambers Building

University Park, Pa 16802

(814) 865-1499 (814) 865-0488 (fax) 814-865-0489 *axj119@*

psu.edu Thank you.

Pilot Course Student Reflections

According to one student participant:

I've come to realize that unless one's education is thorough, it is not an education at all. It may be learning or perhaps experience, but in order to have an education, one must broaden his understanding and have a deep desire to heighten it. I took the pilot course ED197A this past summer and after 6 weeks of interacting with different groups of people, I feel that I am developing a better understanding and awareness of others' perspectives. Andrew Jackson's course was centered on daily presentations by individuals from many different communities, the curriculum, as well as other resources. We got a glimpse into the point of view of a local faculty/administrator out lesbian, watched a Japanese Tea Ceremony and got a brief introduction to East

Indian culture and ideology and was introduced to Muslim Religion and Customs . Whether it was a Rabbi discussing Judaism or a Penn State administrator or faculty member confronting the Media's portrayal of African Americans in Advertising and Commercials, each day's agenda was certain to be enlightening and challenging. Most importantly, at the end of each class we were asked to reflect on what we felt and how our own perspective had been expanded. Frankly, there are thousands of Penn State students who need to experience practical diversity. In the wake of the "Village" (a student protest in the Hub- Robeson Building at Penn State, 2001), it's obvious that the educational needs of many people are not being met without even a brief exposure to the perspectives of other people, people starving for an education will not even be aware of the need for it. I thank the College of Education for such a unique opportunity to deepen my education and trust that more students will be able to experience the course in the future (Junior).

A senior student had the following reaction:

Although multicultural education can be defined and approached from many different angles, intrinsic in all these is the investigation of different perspectives. As Andrew Jackson, Sr. stated throughout the course, "the definition of multicultural that I have come to understand over the last several weeks includes, learning to recognize and accept others' viewpoints and to see that there is value in each person's viewpoints, and to see that there is value in each group's story. By being taught in a way that respects the difference perspectives that can be taken on ant subject, we can develop deeper understandings of both the topic at hand and each other.

Another said:

There is one topic that arises almost daily in class that I have felt confused about from the beginning, what it means to identify with a particular ethnicity. On the very first day we went around the room and shared our names, backgrounds, and identities. I was a little dumbfounded when it was my turn to share. I can't remember ever thinking of myself as apart of a particular ethnic group, (other than as vaguely as a White American). My grandparents on my mother's side has a variety of different heritages, but to call myself Ukrainian American would mean about as much to me as calling myself a Penn State Student American. Sure, some aspect of me is associated with these places and cultures but I've never thought about their influence in defining who I am as a person. Therefore, I have had trouble understanding other people's pull towards an ethnicity as part of who they are. This especially true, when the pull is toward an ethnicity that they had never been exposed to as children, due to some other oppressive culture.

Another student said:

When I ponder why I have not thought about myself as a part of an ethnicity, I believe it is partially related to the atmosphere in which I have lived. I grew up in an almost entirely White European American, upper middle class township, where I was part of a racial White majority. Most of my friends, I'm sure would also have identified themselves vaguely, as White Americans. Perhaps, that was sufficient because we felt that our experiences as middle–class White males was well represented. It's not a secret that media, educational systems, and mainstream politics are geared toward this particular group. To a lesser extent, this is also true at Penn state. For instance, in my entire academic career, including three years at Penn State, Andrew Jackson, is the first non- White teacher/professor that I have ever had! Even in academia, I have usually not had to "think outside the box". So to speak!

According to one of the participants in this study:

Over the duration of the class, I feel like I have developed a much deeper appreciation for why it is important to identify with and take pride in an ethnicity. For one thing, different heritages and cultures offer different and insightful perspectives on social, economic, and political issues. These different perspectives can be very helpful when trying to understand a topic holistically. Different ethnic cultures are also expressions of different types of experiences and it is easy to see that one ethnic identity (such as American or "White American" or "person of color") is not sufficient to explain the struggles and conditions of many groups of people. These groups of people, though co-existing in the same nation, have vastly different experiences. This personal situation that I have described is an example of the kind of learning that takes place in multicultural education. Through exposure of people of so many different backgrounds and cultures in class, I feel that I have gained a much better understanding of different view points, I have a stronger appreciation of their value. Of course, I already had an appreciation for other's experiences and perspectives or I would not have taken this course, but learning takes place when you are surrounded by people who hold these stories (and not just reading about them in a textbook) is great.

In a variety of presentations we have had and the variety of speakers who have shared with our class, I think that one point has stood out to me the most. This was when our senior diversity specialist stated that when it comes to discussing these issues of race, religion, gender, sex, ethnicity, etc., it really is a "heart thing, not a head thing". This phrase says a lot! Multicultural Education (MCE) is responsible for educating our hearts and not just our minds. Through familiarity and understanding of people who come from different backgrounds and experiences than ourselves, we are not just acquiring knowledge but wisdom too. The wisdom that we all share feelings of love, pain, fear, hope, etc. just molded by our different experiences. That we think or are taught otherwise is our folly.

The students and guest speakers shared their reflections after each class. Additional facilitation strategies used included the ethnographic research observations, classroom interviews, survey instrument and content analysis of human interest stories, videotapes, textbooks, articles, and group presentations from the "Village" (students who participated in the 2001 Sit In) and group presentations from the Interfaith Community Coalition Against Prejudice and Violence (community members reacting to the HUB Robeson Sit In 2001).

Summary

The Saturday, March 31, 2001 Statewide Spring Conference at the Penn Stater Conference Institute was another activity that allowed students, faculty, staff, and community members to share feed back on their perspective of race, ethnicity, and diversity issues in preparation for the study and the pilot class. The conference was co- sponsored by the Office of Equity Education, College of Education, Office of Undergraduate Education and the Office of Outreach and Continuing Education. The conference, "Measuring Diversity in a Climate of Change", was also a venue to identify problems that needed to be addressed in pre-service training of teachers and looking at curriculum integration and reform models. The conference was also a precursor to the summer research and diversity pilot course used to implement the pilot course ED 197A: A Dialogue in Race, Ethnicity, Sex, Religion, Gender, and Diversity Issues in Education and Community, including the theoretical support for the focus groups. The Keynote address was by the speaker from the North Carolina State University, Ashville, North Carolina; the address, by Dean of the College of Education and the participation of the College of Education Climate Committee Chairs, the Director of the Office Multicultural Affairs, the Vice President for Student Services the Executive Secretary of the National Association of

Multicultural Education, the Vice Provost for Undergraduate Education and the Vice Provost for Equity Issues. The conference organizer was Andrew Jackson, Sr. The program was videotaped by James Rossi of C-Net (Community Access Television) in State College, Pennsylvania.

Letter of Consent

Page 1 of 1

IMPLIED RN-FORMED CONSENT FORM FOR SOCIAL SCIENCE RESEARCH	ORP USE ONLY: The Pennsylvania state University Office for Research Protections Approval Date: 10/1/03 – J. Mathieu Expiration date: 9/13/04 – J. Mathieu Social Science Institutional Review Board

The Pennsylvania State University

Title of Project	Multicultural Education Pilot Survey Instrument
Principal Investigator:	Andrew Jackson, Sr., Penn State University College of Education, 228 Chambers Building University Park, PA 16802 (814) 238-1666/865-0488 Email- *axj119@psu.edu*

Advisor: Dr. Edgar Farmer, Penn State University,
College of Education, 411 Keller Building
University Park, PA 16802, (814) 863-3858
Email: *eif1@psu.edu*

1. Propose of the Study: The purpose of this research study is to explore students' perception of the need for an additional multicultural education or diversity course at Penn State and in the College of Education. Also of interest is how students understand the need for additional courses in multicultural education or diversity

2. Procedures to be followed: Students will be asked to answer 15 questions on a survey to determine their perception on whether race, gender, and ethnicity effects their teaching style as a teacher

3. Discomforts and Risks: There are no risks in participating in this research beyond these experienced in everyday life. Some of the questions are personal and might cause discomfort

4. Benefits:

   a. You might learn more about yourself by participating in this study. You might have a better understanding of diversity and multicultural education. You might realize that others. have- had similar experiences as you have in understanding the need and purpose for multicultural education and diversity in the curriculum

b. This research might provide a better understanding of how of multicultural education and diversity affect college student. This information could give students an opportunity to learn about other groups' cross-cultural experiences in society. This information might assist students in exploring global awareness of intercultural and inter group relations.

5. Duration: It will take about 10 minutes to complete the questions.

6. Statement of Confidentiality: The survey does not ask for any information that would identify who the responses belong to. Therefore, your responses are recorded anonymously. If this research is published, no information that would identify you will be written since your name is in no way linked to your responses.

7. Right to Ask Questions: Yon can ask questions about the research. The person in charge will answer your questions. Contact Andrew Jackson, Sr., at 814–865–1499 or 814–865–0488 with questions. If you have questions about your rights as a research participant contact Penn State's Office far Research Protection at (814) 865–1775

8. Compensation: Participants will not receive any additional compensation, which might bias or prejudice the student responses.

9. Voluntary Participation: You do not have to participate in this research. Yon can stop your participation at any time. You do not have to answer any questions you do not want to answer.

You must be 18 years of age or older to consent to participate in this research study. Completion and return of the survey applies that you have read the information in this form and consent to participate in the research.

Please keep this form for your records. or future reference.

Pilot Diversity Course Syllabus

February 26, 2001.

New Course Proposal: Summer Session #1: Monday, May 14 thru. Friday, June 22, 2001.

A. *Multicultural Perspectives in Education*
1. Abbreviation: ED
2. Number: 197A
3. Title: *Multicultural Perspectives-in Education*
4. Abbreviated title (18 bytes or less): *Multic Perspect Ed*
5. This course is proposed as a required multicultural education or diversity elective (humanities or social behavioral) course

6. Credits: 3cr.
7. Description (20 words or less): **This course focuses on current literature in multicultural education, discussing race, sex, ethnicity, gender, and religion in education.**
8. Prerequisite (s) -

B. *Course Outline*

1. A brief outline of the course content (1)African Americans (Blacks, People of Color), (2) Asians, (3) Hispanics (Latinos, Puerto Ricans, Cubans, North, South, Central Americans, Caribbeans, Jamaicans, etc.); (4) Native Americans, (5) European Whites (Anglos), (6) other National and ethnically represented groups in America) (7) (Banks, 1995) Teaching Strategies for Ethnic Studies. (8) Multicultural Education as an Academic Discipline, (9) Gender Issues, (10) Religious Differences (Muslim, Jewish, Christian, Baptist, Methodist, etc.)

2. **This course, developed by Andrew Jackson, Sr., will focus on the current literature in the multicultural education annual edition and discuss race, sex, ethnicity, religion, and gender issues in education. The course is designed to give educators and other community members an opportunity to discuss ways of achieving, understanding, and**

promoting multicultural education and diversity in education. It is intended for students, faculty, staff, administrators, social workers, elementary and secondary educators, librarians, school personnel, business and industry personnel, and other community. citizens. A pre-and post survey will be administered to measure and evaluate the objectives of increasing understanding and awareness of multicultural education perspectives.

3. The required text for the course is the seventh edition (or more recent) of the Multicultural Education Annual (ex. 2000–2001) edited by Fred Schultz, University of Akron, Akron, Ohio. Dushkin/McGraw Hill Publishers. Guilford, Connecticut

4. Course Description:

The concept of multicultural education evolved and took shape in the United States out of the social turmoil that wrenched the nation in the late 1960's through the 1970's and 1980's, and into the present decade. The critical literature on gender, race, and culture in educational studies increases our knowledge base regarding the multicultural mosaic that so richly adorns North American cultures. Educators who taught in this area in the past had to draw heavily from academic literatures in anthropology, sociology, social psychology, social history, socio-linguistics, and psychiatry, etc

The course reviews this history, addresses current, related issues, and helps registrants reflect on their own related values to then focus on an individual's roles in fostering a diversity receptive community climate.

5. *Andrew Jackson, Sr., Instructor of Education*–Course Developer

C. *Justification Statement*:

1. **The objectives of this course are to address multicultural issues of race, sex, ethnicity, class, religion, and gender perspectives. The course is designed to eve educators and other community members an opportunity to discuss ways of achieving, understanding, and promoting multicultural education and diversity. Another objective is to engage the registrants, i.e.: staff, faculty, administrators, social workers, elementary, and secondary educators, business and industry personnel, parents, and other citizens in classroom and out of class dialogues focused on the pertinent literature and on their own cross cultural experiences concern-**

ing multicultural education issues and perspectives. Citing the works of James A. Banks and other scholars, multicultural perspectives will add considerable substance to the socio-cultural foundations of education and leadership.

The accreditation standards of the National Council for the Accreditation of Teacher Education (NCATE) requires that accredited teacher education programs offer course content in multicultural education. A global concept of the subject is recommended, in which prospective educators are encouraged to develop cultural sensitivity to the demographic changes and cultural diversity that continue to develop in the public schools and elsewhere in the community as a result of dramatic demographic shifts. (Fred Schultz).

2. *Evaluation Methods:* The evaluation measures include: Quizzes (**10%**), Mid-Term (**25%**), Final, Paper (**25%**), presentations (**10%**), Readings, Reports, special projects agreed upon (**10%**), and Attendance and class participation (**20%**).

3. Quizzes (short pop quizzes)(10%)
4. Mid Term (25%)
5. Final Paper (25%)
6. Presentations (10%)
7. Special Projects (10%)

8. Attendance and Class Participation (20%)

Every student should strive for an A. Assignments are weighted as follows:

Grading Weighted:
A=90–100%, B=89–80%, C=79–70%, D=69–61%,
F=Below 61%

(Students will have pre-approved contracts for special projects such as video or group presentation., power point presentation, sharing additional resources; etc.

Grading:

A (all assignments complete, no absences, special project shared, above 90%)

(all assignments completed after revisions discussed voluntarily, special project completed).

(all assignments completed after revisions and special projects, one excused absence)

B   (All assignments completed satisfactorily, one excused absence, no special project)above 80%

(All assignments completed with no corrections after revisions-two excused absences, no special project)

(all assignments completed, minimum errors, quiz results satisfactory, no special project completed, two excused absences)

C   (all assignments completed with minimum corrections after revisions, no special project, two excused absences) above 70%

(minimal competency demonstrated before corrections and discussion., no special project completed)

(two unexcused absences, incomplete assignments, deficient research, special project)

D   (two unexcused absences, poor scholarship, deficient research skills, and incomplete assignments, no special project) above 61%

F-below 61% (no participation and three unexcused absences, no special project)

4. Initially the course offering during summer session #1 (May 14 thru June 22, 2001) will enroll 25 to 30 students.

5. This course is proposed as an elective (humanities or social behavioral) course to enable students to assess their impact on the climate of diversity in their community, as well as in society at large.

Recommended Supporting Materials:.

Banks, James A. (1995, 1991) *Teaching Strategies for Ethnic Studies* (5th Ed. or 6th edition) Allyn and Bacon. Nedham Heights, Mass.

Resources for discussing basic instructional problems in

teaching ethnic content and integrating it into the curriculum.

Banks, James A. (1997a) *Educating Citizens in a Multicultural Society.* New York. Teachers College Press.

Banks, James A. (1996) *Multicultural Education, Transformative Knowledge, and Action: Historical and Contemporary* Perspectives. New York Teachers College Press.

Banks, James A. (1997). *A Multiethnic Education: Theory and Practice*, 2nd ed. Boston: Allyn and Bacon.

The author describes theories, paradigms, and strategies for implementing multicultural education.

Banks, James A., and Banks, Cherry McGee. (1995) *Handbook of Research on Multicultural Education.* Macmillan. New York.

James A. Banks., and Banks, Cherry A. McGee, eds. (1997) *Multicultural Education: Issues and Perspectives.* Boston: Allyn and Bacon. Nineteen experts in multicultural education provide diverse perspectives and conceptual frameworks for implementing multicultural education in educational institutions.

Banks, James A. (2001) *Cultural Diversity and Education: Foundations, Curriculum and Teaching* (Fourth edition). Allyn and Bacon. Nedham Heights, Mass.

Dilg, Mary (1999) *Race and Culture in the Classroom: Teaching and Learning Through Multicultural Education.* New York: Teachers College Press.

Derman-Sparks, Louise. (1989) *ABC Task Force. Anti Bias*

Curriculum: Tools for Empowering Young Children. Washington, D. C: National Association for the Education of Young Children.

A book of resources and activities for helping students.

Howard, Gary R. (2001) *We Can't Teach What We Don't Know: White Teachers in Multiracial Schools.* Teachers College Press. New York.

Glazer, Nathan, and Moynihan, Daniel P. (1982) *Beyond the Melting Pot: The Negroes, Puerto Ricans, Jews, Italians and Irish of New York City.* Cambridge, Mass. MIT Press.

Nash, Gary B. (1982) *Red, White, and Black: The Peoples of Early America.* Englewood Cliffs, NJ. Prentice Hall.

Nieto, Sonia. (1999) *The Light in Their Eyes: Creating Multicultural Learning Communities.* New York Teachers College Press.

Takaki, Ronald (1982). *Strangers from a Different Shore: A History of Asian Americans. Boston:* Little, Brown.

Tatum, Beverly Daniel (1997) *Why Are All the Black Kids Sitting Together in the Cafeteria?*, New York Basic Books.

Watkins, William H., Lewis, James H., Chou, Victoria. (2001) *Race and Education: The Roles of History and Society in Educating African American Students.* Allyn and Bacon.

Zinn, Howard, and Kirshner, G. (1995) *A People's History of the United States: The Wall Chart.* New York: The New Press.

Andrew Jackson, Sr., has been an academic advisor for 20 years. He is the past regional #3 director of the National Association of Multicultural Education and president of Penn State University Phi Delta Kappa International chapter #0043 (Alpha Tau). He is also past president of Central PA Local 660  Musicians of the International American Federation of Musicians of the United States and Canada., and plays Fridays at Tony's Big Easy and Saturdays at Beulah's Bar Bleu in Happy Valley (State College, Pennsylvania). A 2003 Leadership Centre County member, and a (Rural Urban Leadership Educational Fellow) RULE Class 2005 Dr. Jackson completed his doctorate in multicultural education in February 2004 in the Graduate School Interdisciplinary Graduate Studies Program at Penn State University in the Penn State University Graduate School with Dr. Edgar Farmer, Workforce Education, College of Education, Dr. Henry A. Giroux, former Waterbury Chair in Cultural Studies, College of Education, Dr. James B. Stewart, Economics and African Studies, College of Liberal Arts, Dr. Barbara Pennypacker, Agronomy, College of Agriculture, and Dr. David McBride, African and African-American Studies, College of Liberal Arts.

Printed in the United States
80936LV00002B/152

9 781587 367199